Basic Addition Facts to 18

> Turn to each section to find a more detailed skills list.

Table of Contents

What Does This Book Include?

- More than 80 student practice pages that build basic math skills
- A detailed skills list for each section of the book
- Send-home letters informing parents of the skills being targeted and ways to practice these skills
- Timed student checkups for each addition skill
- A reproducible student progress chart
- Awards to celebrate student progress
- Answer keys for easy checking
- Perforated pages for easy removal and filing if desired

What Are the Benefits of This Book?

- Organized for quick and easy use
- Enhances and supports your existing math program
- Offers six reproducible practice pages for each basic addition skill
- Helps develop mastery of basic facts
- Provides reinforcement for different ability levels
- Includes communication pages that encourage parents' participation in their children's learning of math
- Contains checkups that assess students' addition knowledge
- Offers a reproducible chart for documenting student progress
- Aligns with national math standards

©2004 by THE EDUCATION CENTER, INC.
All rights reserved.
ISBN# 1-56234-581-8

Manufactured in the United States
10 9 8 7 6 5 4 3 2 1

How to Use This Book
Steps to Success

Choose Skills to Target

Scan the detailed table of contents at the beginning of each section to find just the right skills to target your students' needs.

Select Fun Practice Pages

Choose from a variety of fun formats the pages that best match your students' current ability levels.

Fun Formats

Date Skill Completed

Targeted Skill

Letter to Parents Informing Them of Skill to Review

Communicate With Parents

Recruit parent assistance by locating the appropriate parent letter (pages 102–122), making copies, and sending the letter home.

Facts to Practice

Simple At-Home Activity

2

Assess Student Understanding

Assess students' progress with student checkups (mini tests) on pages 103–123. Choose Checkup A or Checkup B.

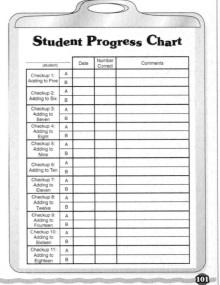

Two Checkups for Each Skill

Document Progress

Documenting student progress can be as easy as 1, 2, 3! Do the following for each student:

1. Make a copy of the Student Progress Chart (page 101).
2. File the chart in his math portfolio or a class notebook.
3. Record the date each checkup is given, the number of correct answers, and any comments regarding his progress.

Celebrate!

Celebrate addition success using the awards on page 124.

Books in the Target Math Success series include

- *Basic Addition Facts to 18*
- *Basic Subtraction Facts to 18*
- *Addition of Larger Numbers*
- *Subtraction of Larger Numbers*
- *Basic Multiplication Facts and More*
- *Basic Division Facts and More*
- *Multiplication of Larger Numbers*
- *Division of Larger Numbers*
- *Fractions*
- *Decimals*

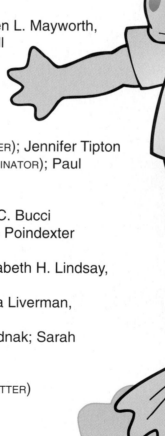

Managing Editor: Deborah G. Swider
Editor at Large: Diane Badden
Staff Editor: Kelly Coder
Copy Editors: Tazmen Carlisle, Amy Kirtley-Hill, Karen L. Mayworth, Kristy Parton, Debbie Shoffner, Cathy Edwards Simrell
Art Coordinator: Pam Crane
Artists: Pam Crane, Theresa Lewis Goode, Clevell Harris, Ivy L. Koonce, Clint Moore, Greg D. Rieves, Rebecca Saunders, Barry Slate, Stuart Smith, Donna K. Teal
The Mailbox® Books.com: Judy P. Wyndham (MANAGER); Jennifer Tipton Bennett (DESIGNER/ARTIST); Karen White (INTERNET COORDINATOR); Paul Fleetwood, Xiaoyun Wu (SYSTEMS)

President, The Mailbox Book Company™: Joseph C. Bucci
Director of Book Planning and Development: Chris Poindexter
Curriculum Director: Karen P. Shelton
Book Development Managers: Cayce Guiliano, Elizabeth H. Lindsay, Thad McLaurin
Editorial Planning: Kimberley Bruck (MANAGER); Debra Liverman, Sharon Murphy, Susan Walker (TEAM LEADERS)
Editorial and Freelance Management: Karen A. Brudnak; Sarah Hamblet, Hope Rodgers (EDITORIAL ASSISTANTS)
Editorial Production: Lisa K. Pitts (TRAFFIC MANAGER); Lynette Dickerson (TYPE SYSTEMS); Mark Rainey (TYPESETTER)
Librarian: Dorothy C. McKinney

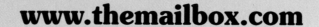

www.themailbox.com

Basic Addition Facts

Basic Addition Facts

Table of Contents

See pages 102–123 for corresponding parent communications and student checkups (mini tests) for the skills listed above.

Heigh-Ho! Off to Work We Go!

Name _____ Date _____

Add.

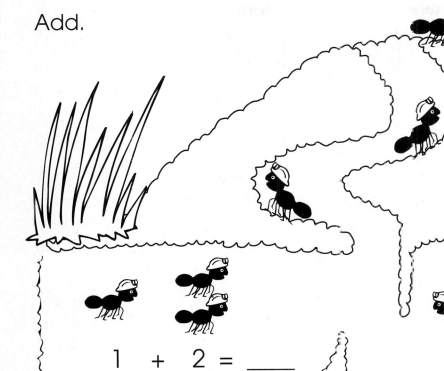

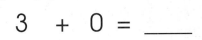

1 + 2 = ___

3 + 0 = ___

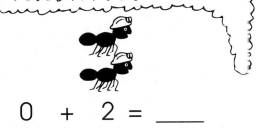

0 + 2 = ___

1 + 1 = ___

1 + 0 = ___

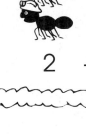

2 + 1 = ___

2 + 0 = ___

0 + 3 = ___

Adding to 3   7

Lip-Licking Good!

Name _____ Date _____

Add.

1 + 1 = ___

0 + 3 = ___

2 + 1 = ___

0 + 2 = ___

1 + 2 = ___

1 + 0 = ___

3 + 0 = ___

0 + 1 = ___

2 + 0 = ___

Field Goal Fun!

Name _____   Date _____

Add.

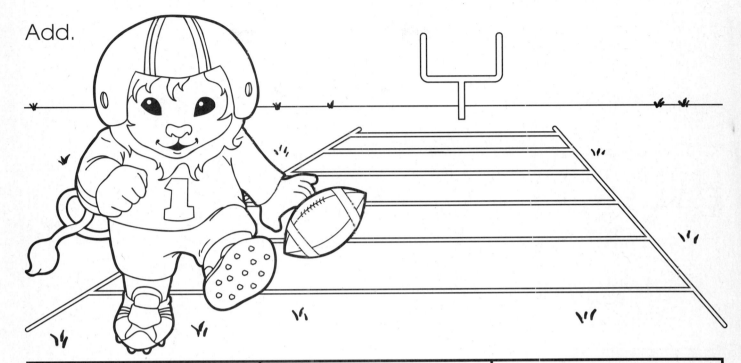

___ + ___ = ___	___ + ___ = ___	___ + ___ = ___
___ + ___ = ___	___ + ___ = ___	___ + ___ = ___
___ + ___ = ___	___ + ___ = ___	___ + ___ = ___

Colorful Facts

Name _____ Date _____

Add.
Color by the code.

2 + 0 = ____   1 + 0 = ____

1 + 2 = ____   2 + 2 = ____

4 + 0 = ____   0 + 2 = ____

0 + 1 = ____   2 + 1 = ____

1 + 1 = ____   3 + 1 = ____

3 + 0 = ____   1 + 0 = ____

Color Code

1—green   2—orange
3—red   4—yellow

CRAYONS

Honey, I'm Home!

Name _____ Date _____

Add.

Help Bee get the honey home.

If the answer is **3** or **4**, color the cell **yellow**.

2 + 1 = __   4 + 0 = __   2 + 0 = __

1 + 1 = __   0 + 1 = __   0 + 2 = __   1 + 3 = __

2 + 2 = __   3 + 1 = __   0 + 3 = __   1 + 0 = __

0 + 4 = __   1 + 1 = __   0 + 0 = __   2 + 0 = __   1 + 1 = __

3 + 0 = __   1 + 2 = __   1 + 3 = __   0 + 0 = __

0 + 1 = __   0 + 2 = __   1 + 0 = __   2 + 1 = __

HONEY

In the Moonlight

Name _____ Date _____

Add.
Color by the code.

$$\begin{array}{r} 0 \\ +1 \\ \hline \end{array}$$

$$\begin{array}{r} 1 \\ +2 \\ \hline \end{array}$$

$$\begin{array}{r} 3 \\ +1 \\ \hline \end{array}$$

$$\begin{array}{r} 1 \\ +1 \\ \hline \end{array}$$

$$\begin{array}{r} 2 \\ +0 \\ \hline \end{array}$$

$$\begin{array}{r} 0 \\ +2 \\ \hline \end{array}$$

$$\begin{array}{r} 1 \\ +3 \\ \hline \end{array}$$

$$\begin{array}{r} 4 \\ +0 \\ \hline \end{array}$$

$$\begin{array}{r} 0 \\ +1 \\ \hline \end{array}$$

$$\begin{array}{r} 1 \\ +0 \\ \hline \end{array}$$

$$\begin{array}{r} 2 \\ +2 \\ \hline \end{array}$$

$$\begin{array}{r} 1 \\ +1 \\ \hline \end{array}$$

$$\begin{array}{r} 2 \\ +1 \\ \hline \end{array}$$

$$\begin{array}{r} 0 \\ +4 \\ \hline \end{array}$$

Sun-Loving Lizards

Name _____ Date _____

Add.

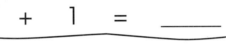

3 + 1 = _____   1 + 4 = _____

1 + 2 = _____   0 + 3 = _____

0 + 5 = _____   2 + 2 = _____

1 + 3 = _____   2 + 3 = _____

2 + 0 = _____   4 + 0 = _____

3 + 2 = _____   2 + 1 = _____

Captain Quacker's Ship

Name _____ Date _____

Add.
Color by the code.

2 + 2 = ___

3 + 1 = ___

0 + 2 = ___

2 + 1 = ___   0 + 3 = ___

3 + 0 = ___   1 + 2 = ___

3 + 1 = ___

Color Code

1—orange
2—purple
3—yellow
4—red
5—blue

0 + 5 = ___   1 + 4 = ___

2 + 3 = ___   3 + 2 = ___

4 + 1 = ___   5 + 0 = ___

3 + 2 = ___   2 + 3 = ___

1 + 0 = ___   0 + 1 = ___

Squirrel's Super-size Snack

Name _____   Date _____

Add.

Help Squirrel get to the big acorn.

If the answer is **3** or **4,** color the box **green.**

1 + 2 = ___	4 + 0 = ___	2 + 3 = ___	3 + 2 = ___
0 + 5 = ___	2 + 2 = ___	1 + 4 = ___	1 + 1 = ___
1 + 0 = ___	1 + 3 = ___	2 + 1 = ___	5 + 0 = ___
3 + 2 = ___	4 + 1 = ___	3 + 0 = ___	0 + 4 = ___

In Full Bloom

Name _____ Date _____

Add.

Color by the code.

Color Code
2—green   3—red
4—blue   5—yellow

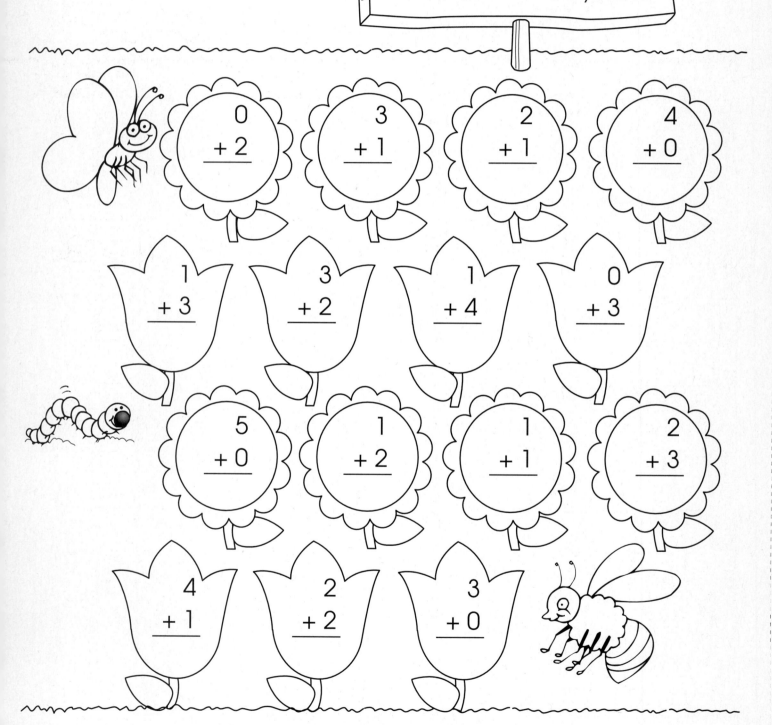

0
+2

3
+1

2
+1

4
+0

1
+3

3
+2

1
+4

0
+3

5
+0

1
+2

1
+1

2
+3

4
+1

2
+2

3
+0

Munch Buddies

Name _____ Date _____

Add.
Color the matching number of peanuts.

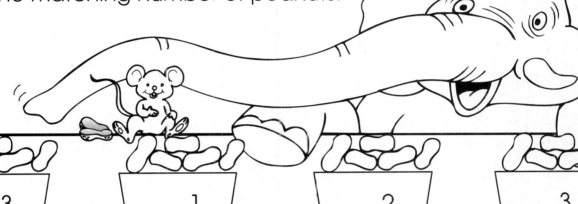

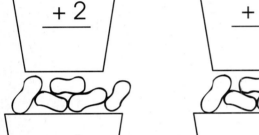

$$3 \atop +2$$

$$1 \atop +4$$

$$2 \atop +2$$

$$3 \atop +0$$

$$1 \atop +1$$

$$5 \atop +0$$

$$4 \atop +1$$

$$1 \atop +3$$

$$0 \atop +5$$

$$1 \atop +2$$

$$2 \atop +3$$

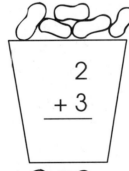

$$4 \atop +0$$

$$2 \atop +1$$

$$0 \atop +3$$

$$2 \atop +0$$

$$3 \atop +1$$

Going for a Swim

Name _____ Date _____

Add.

Remember: Adding two numbers in a different **order** does not change the sum.

1 + 0 = ___
0 + 1 = ___

2 + 0 = ___
0 + 2 = ___

5 + 0 = ___
0 + 5 = ___

0 + 4 = ___
4 + 0 = ___

3 + 1 = ___
1 + 3 = ___

0 + 3 = ___
3 + 0 = ___

1 + 2 = ___
2 + 1 = ___

2 + 3 = ___
3 + 2 = ___

Turn-around facts: adding to 5

Gumball Surprises

Name _____ Date _____

Add.
Color by the code.

$3 + 1 =$ ____

$0 + 1 =$ ____

$2 + 3 =$ ____

$2 + 4 =$ ____

$5 + 0 =$ ____

$2 + 1 =$ ____

$5 + 1 =$ ____

$0 + 6 =$ ____

$2 + 2 =$ ____

$1 + 1 =$ ____

$3 + 2 =$ ____

$4 + 1 =$ ____

$3 + 3 =$ ____

$1 + 3 =$ ____

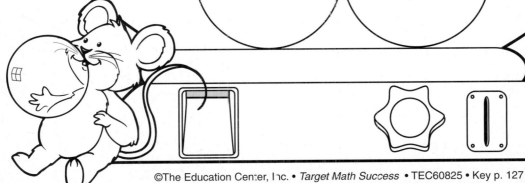

Wh re's My Bon ?

Name _____ Date _____

Add.

Help Max find his bone.

If the answer is **5** or **6**, color the box **green**.

6 + 0	4 + 1

0 + 3	2 + 2	2 + 3
5 + 1	3 + 3	0 + 5
2 + 4	1 + 3	1 + 1
1 + 4	0 + 6	

Garden Helper

Name _____ Date _____

Add.
Color by the code.

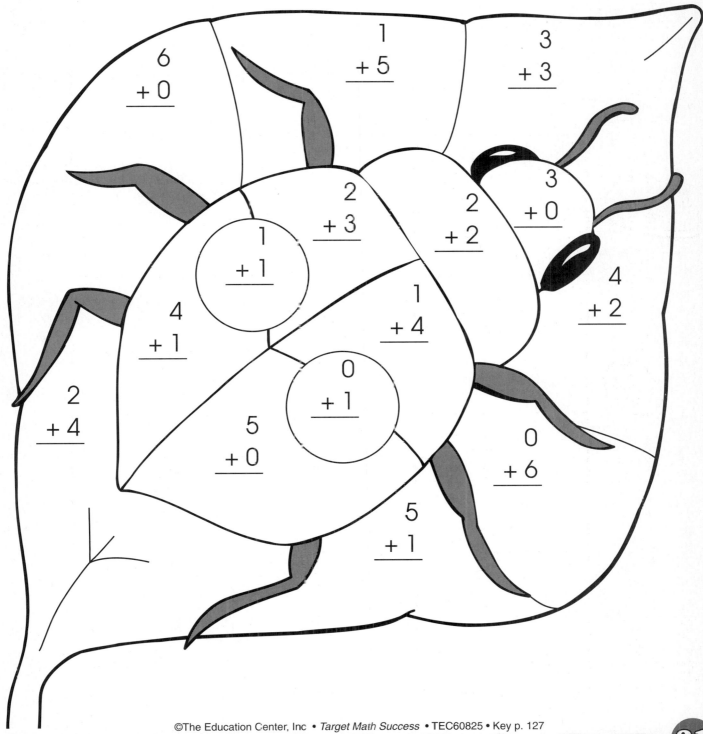

Making a Splash

Name _____ Date _____

Add.
Color by the code.

$$\begin{array}{r} 2 \\ +3 \\ \hline \end{array}$$

$$\begin{array}{r} 5 \\ +1 \\ \hline \end{array}$$

$$\begin{array}{r} 3 \\ +2 \\ \hline \end{array}$$

$$\begin{array}{r} 2 \\ +4 \\ \hline \end{array}$$

$$\begin{array}{r} 5 \\ +1 \\ \hline \end{array}$$

$$\begin{array}{r} 0 \\ +6 \\ \hline \end{array}$$

$$\begin{array}{r} 1 \\ +4 \\ \hline \end{array}$$

$$\begin{array}{r} 1 \\ +0 \\ \hline \end{array}$$

$$\begin{array}{r} 0 \\ +1 \\ \hline \end{array}$$

$$\begin{array}{r} 0 \\ +5 \\ \hline \end{array}$$

$$\begin{array}{r} 4 \\ +1 \\ \hline \end{array}$$

$$\begin{array}{r} 4 \\ +2 \\ \hline \end{array}$$

$$\begin{array}{r} 3 \\ +3 \\ \hline \end{array}$$

$$\begin{array}{r} 1 \\ +1 \\ \hline \end{array}$$

$$\begin{array}{r} 3 \\ +1 \\ \hline \end{array}$$

$$\begin{array}{r} 1 \\ +2 \\ \hline \end{array}$$

$$\begin{array}{r} 2 \\ +2 \\ \hline \end{array}$$

$$\begin{array}{r} 4 \\ +0 \\ \hline \end{array}$$

Color Code
1—pink   2, 3, or 4—yellow   5 or 6—blue

In the "Moo-d" for Ice Cream

Name _____   Date _____

Read.
Write the math sentence.

Cow eats **2** s.

She eats **2 more**.

How many 🍦s **in all**?

_____ + _____ = _____

Cow has **2** 🧁s.

She makes **3 more**.

How many 🧁s **in all**?

_____ + _____ = _____

Cow makes **5** s.

She makes **1 more**.

How many 🥤s **in all**?

_____ + _____ = _____

Cow has **3** 🍨s.

She buys **3 more**.

How many 🍨s **in all**?

_____ + _____ = _____

Cow has **2** 🍫s.

She eats **4 more**.

How many 🍫s **in all**?

_____ + _____ = _____

Cow has **4** 🍒s.

She gets **1 more**.

How many 🍒s **in all**?

_____ + _____ = _____

Party Under the Sea

Name _____ Date _____

Read.

Write the math sentence.

5 crabs have hats. 1 fish has a hat. How many hats in all? _____ + _____ = _____	2 fish dance. 3 more fish dance. How many fish in all? _____ + _____ = _____
1 sea horse swims by. 4 more sea horses swim by. How many sea horses in all? _____ + _____ = _____	3 crabs sing. 3 more crabs sing. How many crabs in all? _____ + _____ = _____
There are 2 green plants. There are 4 red plants. How many plants in all? _____ + _____ = _____	There are 3 blue shells. There is 1 yellow shell. How many shells in all? _____ + _____ = _____

Banana Fort Buddies

Name _____   Date _____

Add.
Color by the code.

$6 + 1 =$ _____

$1 + 4 =$ _____

$2 + 2 =$ _____

$3 + 2 =$ _____

$0 + 5 =$ _____

$4 + 0 =$ _____

$5 + 2 =$ _____

$1 + 3 =$ _____

$3 + 4 =$ _____

$1 + 5 =$ _____

$7 + 0 =$ _____

$2 + 5 =$ _____

$0 + 7 =$ _____

$3 + 3 =$ _____

$0 + 6 =$ _____

$4 + 2 =$ _____

$1 + 6 =$ _____

$4 + 3 =$ _____

$0 + 4 =$ _____

$5 + 0 =$ _____

$2 + 3 =$ _____

$4 + 1 =$ _____

©The Education Center, Inc. • *Target Math Success* • TEC60825 • Key p. 128

Mouse's Midnight Munchies

Name _____   Date _____

Add.

Help hungry Mouse find the cheese.

If the answer is **6** or **7**, color the box **yellow**.

0 +3	6 +1	1 +5	4 +1	2 +3
1 +4	3 +1	3 +3	5 +0	2 +1
2 +2	3 +2	7 +0	2 +5	0 +6
0 +4	1 +3	0 +5	4 +0	4 +3

©The Education Center, Inc. • *Target Math Success* • TEC60825 • Key p. 128

26 **Adding to 7**

Honey, Sweet Honey

Name _____ Date _____

Add.
Color by the code.

Color Code	
4—purple	6—blue
5—red	7—yellow

$$4 + 3$$ $$2 + 3$$ $$7 + 0$$ $$1 + 4$$ $$2 + 5$$

$$3 + 3$$ $$5 + 2$$ $$2 + 4$$ $$6 + 1$$ $$2 + 2$$

$$3 + 4$$ $$1 + 3$$ $$1 + 6$$ $$4 + 0$$ $$5 + 1$$

I ♥ HONEY

HONEY

B rny rd Hide- nd-Se k

Name _____ Date _____

Add.
Color by the code.

0 +3	1 +2

2 +1	1 +0	0 +2	0 +1

1 +6

1 +1	2 +0	3 +0	1 +0

7 +0

0 +4		3 +2

2 +4	3 +3

3 +4

6 +1

0 +7

4 +3	1 +5	2 +5	5 +2

6 +0	0 +6

1, 2, 3, 4,
5, 6, 7...

What a Smile!

Name _____ Date _____

Read.
Add.
Color by the code.

How many muscles does it take to smile?

| 7
+0 | 6
+1 | 2
+5 | 1
+5 |

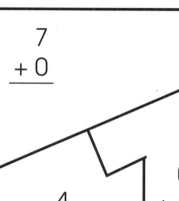
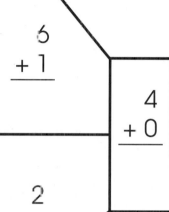

4
+0

4
+2   0
+4   2
+3   1
+2   4
+1

4
+3

| 3
+2 | 3
+4 | 3
+0 | 3
+3 | 1
+4 | 1
+3 | 5
+2 |

0
+5   5
+0

5
+1   6
+0   0
+7   2
+4

Repeat After Me

Name _____ Date _____

Add.

Remember:
Adding two numbers in a different **order** does not change the sum.

5 + 2 = ____
2 + 5 = ____

0 + 5 = ____
5 + 0 = ____

2 + 4 = ____
4 + 2 = ____

0 + 6 = ____
6 + 0 = ____

0 + 3 = ____
3 + 0 = ____

7 + 0 = ____
0 + 7 = ____

1 + 5 = ____
5 + 1 = ____

3 + 1 = ____
1 + 3 = ____

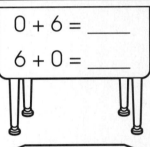

4 + 1 = ____
1 + 4 = ____

0 + 2 = ____
2 + 0 = ____

4 + 3 = ____
3 + 4 = ____

1 + 2 = ____
2 + 1 = ____

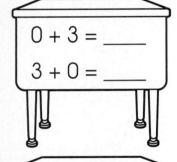

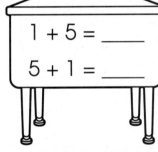

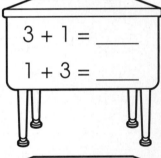

0 + 1 = ____
1 + 0 = ____

2 + 3 = ____
3 + 2 = ____

4 + 0 = ____
0 + 4 = ____

1 + 6 = ____
6 + 1 = ____

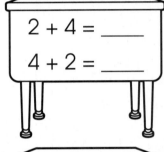

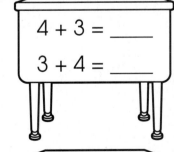

Cookie Creatures

Name _____   Date _____

Read each big number.
Circle 4 ways to make that number.

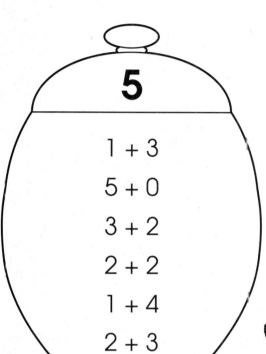

5

1 + 3
5 + 0
3 + 2
2 + 2
1 + 4
2 + 3

6

0 + 6
1 + 5
4 + 1
4 + 2
1 + 1
3 + 3

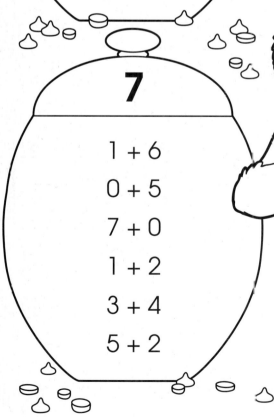

7

1 + 6
0 + 5
7 + 0
1 + 2
3 + 4
5 + 2

8

2 + 5
1 + 7
6 + 2
4 + 0
4 + 4
3 + 5

Fun in the Sun

Name _____   Date _____

Add.
Color by the code.

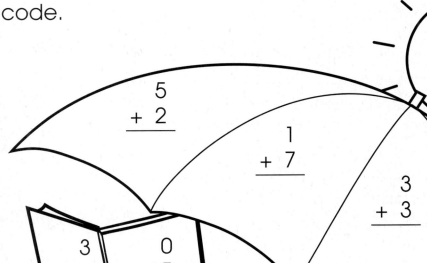

$$\begin{array}{r} 2 \\ + 4 \\ \hline \end{array}$$

$$\begin{array}{r} 5 \\ + 2 \\ \hline \end{array}$$

$$\begin{array}{r} 1 \\ + 7 \\ \hline \end{array}$$

$$\begin{array}{r} 3 \\ + 3 \\ \hline \end{array}$$

$$\begin{array}{r} 4 \\ + 1 \\ \hline \end{array}$$

$$\begin{array}{r} 3 \\ + 2 \\ \hline \end{array}$$

$$\begin{array}{r} 0 \\ + 5 \\ \hline \end{array}$$

$$\begin{array}{r} 2 \\ + 2 \\ \hline \end{array}$$

$$\begin{array}{r} 6 \\ + 2 \\ \hline \end{array}$$

$$\begin{array}{r} 3 \\ + 1 \\ \hline \end{array}$$

$$\begin{array}{r} 5 \\ + 1 \\ \hline \end{array}$$

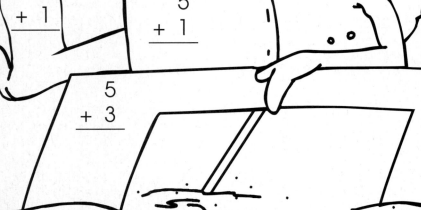

$$\begin{array}{r} 5 \\ + 3 \\ \hline \end{array}$$

$$\begin{array}{r} 0 \\ + 8 \\ \hline \end{array}$$

Color Code

4—brown
5—green
6—yellow
7—blue
8—red

$$\begin{array}{r} 1 \\ + 6 \\ \hline \end{array}$$

$$\begin{array}{r} 3 \\ + 4 \\ \hline \end{array}$$

What's Poppin'?

Name _____   Date _____

Add.

If the answer is **8**, color it **yellow**.

Picnic Path

Name _____ Date _____

Add.

Help the ant find the food.

If the answer is **7** or **8**, color the box **red**.

$\begin{array}{r} 0 \\ + 8 \\ \hline \end{array}$	$\begin{array}{r} 2 \\ + 5 \\ \hline \end{array}$	$\begin{array}{r} 4 \\ + 3 \\ \hline \end{array}$	$\begin{array}{r} 1 \\ + 5 \\ \hline \end{array}$
$\begin{array}{r} 2 \\ + 2 \\ \hline \end{array}$	$\begin{array}{r} 3 \\ + 2 \\ \hline \end{array}$	$\begin{array}{r} 1 \\ + 2 \\ \hline \end{array}$	$\begin{array}{r} 4 \\ + 4 \\ \hline \end{array}$	$\begin{array}{r} 3 \\ + 3 \\ \hline \end{array}$
$\begin{array}{r} 3 \\ + 0 \\ \hline \end{array}$	$\begin{array}{r} 2 \\ + 6 \\ \hline \end{array}$	$\begin{array}{r} 7 \\ + 1 \\ \hline \end{array}$	$\begin{array}{r} 0 \\ + 7 \\ \hline \end{array}$	$\begin{array}{r} 2 \\ + 4 \\ \hline \end{array}$
$\begin{array}{r} 1 \\ + 3 \\ \hline \end{array}$	$\begin{array}{r} 5 \\ + 3 \\ \hline \end{array}$	$\begin{array}{r} 5 \\ + 1 \\ \hline \end{array}$	$\begin{array}{r} 2 \\ + 3 \\ \hline \end{array}$	$\begin{array}{r} 1 \\ + 1 \\ \hline \end{array}$
$\begin{array}{r} 5 \\ + 0 \\ \hline \end{array}$	$\begin{array}{r} 5 \\ + 2 \\ \hline \end{array}$	$\begin{array}{r} 6 \\ + 1 \\ \hline \end{array}$	

I'm hungry!

Camping Camels

Name _____ Date _____

Read.
Write the math sentence.

Carl Camel ate 3 hot dogs. He ate 2 more. How many hot dogs in all? _____ + _____ = _____	Cathy Camel put 4 logs on the fire. She added 2 more. How many logs in all? _____ + _____ = _____
Carl Camel sang 4 songs. He sang 4 more. How many songs in all? _____ + _____ = _____	Cathy Camel caught 3 fish. She caught 4 more. How many fish in all? _____ + _____ = _____
Carl Camel put up 5 tents. He put up 3 more. How many tents in all? _____ + _____ = _____	The camels roasted 6 marshmallows. They roasted 1 more. How many marshmallows in all? _____ + _____ = _____

Story problems: adding to 8 35

Sam the Snoozing Snake

Name _____   Date _____

Read.
Write the math sentence.
Color by the code.

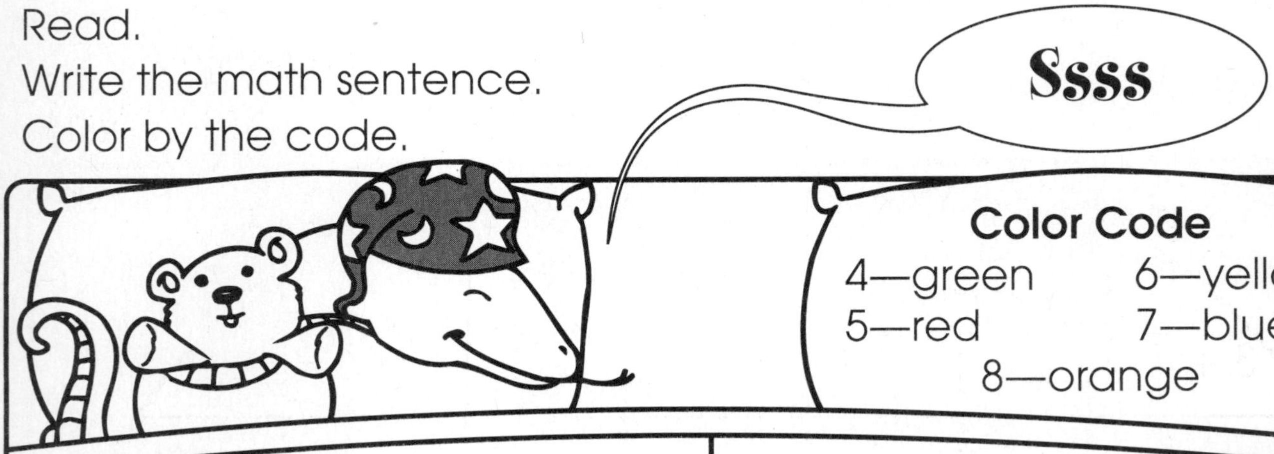

Ssss

Color Code

4—green	6—yellow
5—red	7—blue
8—orange	

Sam sleeps for 4 hours.
He sleeps for 1 more.
How many hours in all?

____ + ____ = ____

There are 2 pillows.
There are 2 more.
How many pillows in all?

____ + ____ = ____

Sam has 2 teddy bears.
He gets 5 more.
How many bears in all?

____ + ____ = ____

Sam crawls 6 inches.
He crawls 2 more.
How many inches in all?

____ + ____ = ____

Sam has 3 brothers.
He has 3 sisters.
How many in all?

____ + ____ = ____

Sam sees 2 mice.
He sees 3 more.
How many mice in all?

____ + ____ = ____

There is 1 red snake.
There are 7 black snakes.
How many snakes in all?

____ + ____ = ____

Sam has 4 dreams.
He has 3 more.
How many dreams in all?

____ + ____ = ____

Story problems: adding to 8

Up, Up, and Away!

Name _____ Date _____

Add.
Color by the code.

$3 + 2 =$ _____

$3 + 5 =$ _____ $1 + 6 =$ _____ $1 + 7 =$ _____

$0 + 9 =$ _____ $8 + 1 =$ _____ $7 + 2 =$ _____

$2 + 6 =$ _____ $3 + 4 =$ _____ $4 + 4 =$ _____

$5 + 4 =$ _____ $6 + 3 =$ _____ $9 + 0 =$ _____

$5 + 3 =$ _____ $7 + 0 =$ _____ $6 + 2 =$ _____

$2 + 7 =$ _____ $4 + 5 =$ _____ $1 + 8 =$ _____

$1 + 5 =$ _____ $2 + 4 =$ _____

$4 + 1 =$ _____

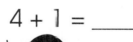

Yummy for My Tummy

Name _____ Date _____

Add.

If the answer is **9**, color the carrot **orange**.

$8 + 1$ $2 + 6$ $4 + 5$ $6 + 1$ $3 + 2$

$5 + 2$ $2 + 7$ $0 + 6$ $4 + 4$ $0 + 9$

$3 + 6$ $9 + 0$ $6 + 2$ $3 + 4$ $1 + 8$

$5 + 4$ $4 + 2$ $3 + 5$ $6 + 3$ $6 + 0$

Look Out Below!

Name _____ Date _____

Add.
Color by the code.

Color Code
9—pink
8—brown
7—green
6—purple
5—red
2, 3, or 4—yellow

$$\begin{array}{r} 4 \\ + 0 \\ \hline \end{array}$$

$$\begin{array}{r} 3 \\ + 1 \\ \hline \end{array}$$

$$\begin{array}{r} 1 \\ + 1 \\ \hline \end{array}$$

$$\begin{array}{r} 1 \\ + 8 \\ \hline \end{array}$$

$$\begin{array}{r} 2 \\ + 0 \\ \hline \end{array}$$

$$\begin{array}{r} 3 \\ + 6 \\ \hline \end{array}$$

$$\begin{array}{r} 5 \\ + 4 \\ \hline \end{array}$$

$$\begin{array}{r} 0 \\ + 3 \\ \hline \end{array}$$

$$\begin{array}{r} 2 \\ + 7 \\ \hline \end{array}$$

$$\begin{array}{r} 2 \\ + 1 \\ \hline \end{array}$$

$$\begin{array}{r} 7 \\ + 1 \\ \hline \end{array}$$

$$\begin{array}{r} 2 \\ + 5 \\ \hline \end{array}$$

$$\begin{array}{r} 6 \\ + 2 \\ \hline \end{array}$$

$$\begin{array}{r} 3 \\ + 5 \\ \hline \end{array}$$

$$\begin{array}{r} 3 \\ + 4 \\ \hline \end{array}$$

$$\begin{array}{r} 6 \\ + 1 \\ \hline \end{array}$$

$$\begin{array}{r} 4 \\ + 4 \\ \hline \end{array}$$

$$\begin{array}{r} 0 \\ + 7 \\ \hline \end{array}$$

$$\begin{array}{r} 1 \\ + 4 \\ \hline \end{array}$$

$$\begin{array}{r} 2 \\ + 3 \\ \hline \end{array}$$

$$\begin{array}{r} 5 \\ + 0 \\ \hline \end{array}$$

$$\begin{array}{r} 6 \\ + 0 \\ \hline \end{array}$$

$$\begin{array}{r} 2 \\ + 4 \\ \hline \end{array}$$

Adding to 9 39

Horse on the Loose!

Add.

Help the cowboy find his horse.

If the answer is **8** or **9**, color the horseshoe **purple**.

3 + 6	0 + 9	4 + 4	2 + 6	1 + 5
5 + 2	4 + 3	6 + 0	4 + 5	6 + 1
1 + 8	3 + 5	8 + 0	7 + 2	3 + 4
9 + 0	2 + 5	5 + 1	1 + 6	3 + 3
1 + 7	6 + 3	5 + 4	2 + 7	8 + 1

Pigs at Work

Name _____ Date _____

Read each big number.
Circle 4 ways to make that number.

6

1 + 5
0 + 4
2 + 1
3 + 3
6 + 0
4 + 2

7

3 + 4
6 + 1
2 + 6
5 + 0
2 + 5
7 + 0

8

1 + 7
5 + 3
2 + 5
1 + 6
4 + 4
6 + 2

9

3 + 6
7 + 1
4 + 5
8 + 1
7 + 2
2 + 6

Lazy Day at the Pond

Name _____ Date _____

Add.

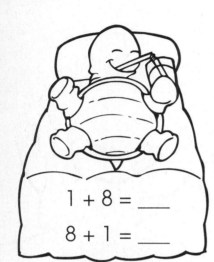

$1 + 8 =$ ___
$8 + 1 =$ ___

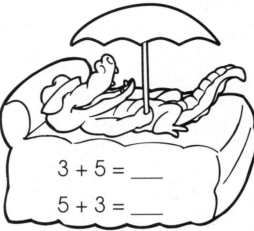

$3 + 5 =$ ___
$5 + 3 =$ ___

$3 + 6 =$ ___
$6 + 3 =$ ___

$4 + 3 =$ ___
$3 + 4 =$ ___

$7 + 2 =$ ___
$2 + 7 =$ ___

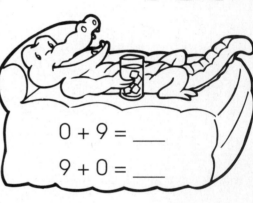

$0 + 9 =$ ___
$9 + 0 =$ ___

$4 + 5 =$ ___
$5 + 4 =$ ___

$5 + 2 =$ ___
$2 + 5 =$ ___

$7 + 1 =$ ___
$1 + 7 =$ ___

Turn-around facts: adding to 9

Smooth Sailing

Name _____   Date _____

Add.
Color by the code.

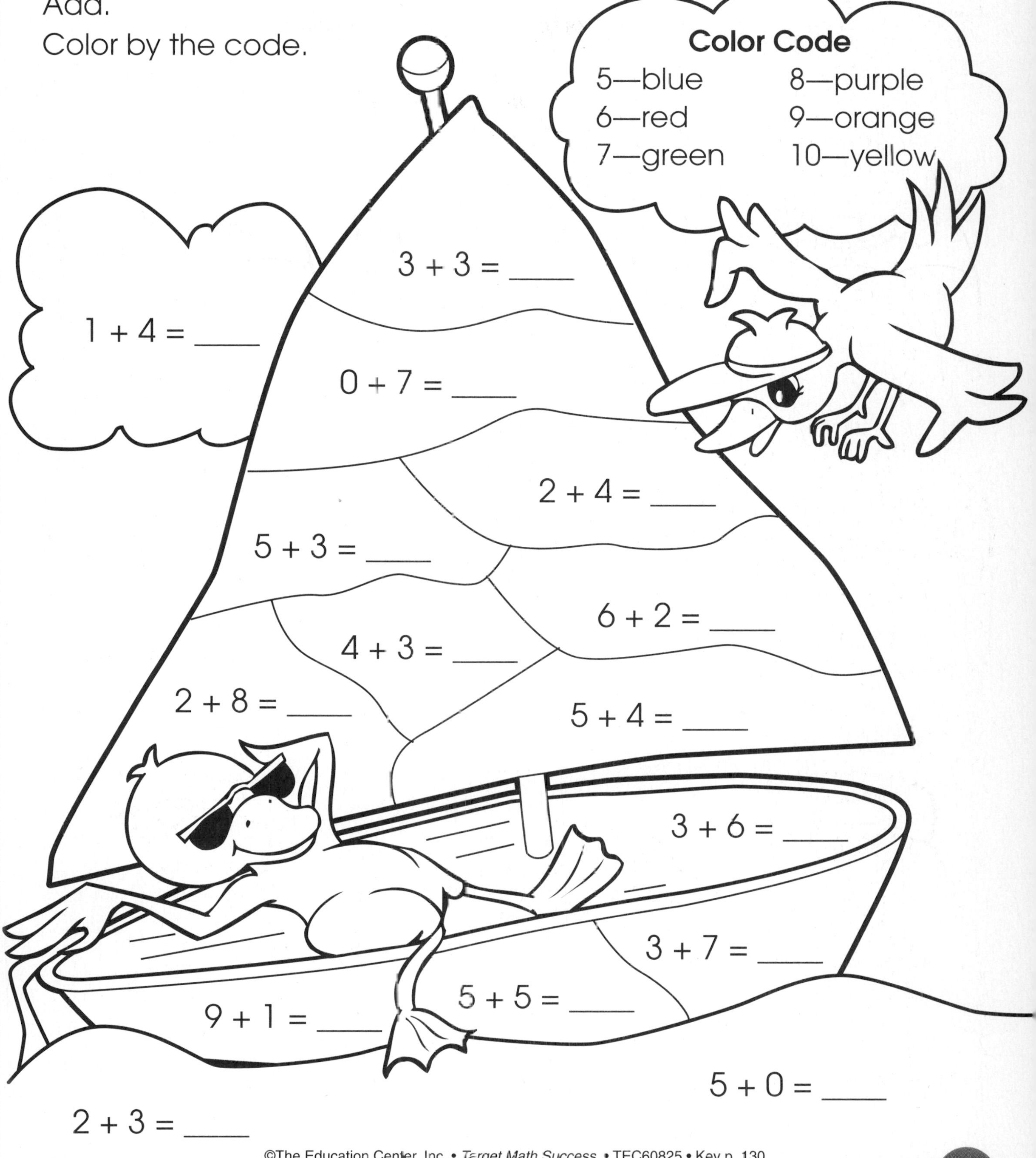

$3 + 3 =$ ____

$1 + 4 =$ ____

$0 + 7 =$ ____

$2 + 4 =$ ____

$5 + 3 =$ ____

$6 + 2 =$ ____

$4 + 3 =$ ____

$2 + 8 =$ ____

$5 + 4 =$ ____

$3 + 6 =$ ____

$3 + 7 =$ ____

$9 + 1 =$ ____

$5 + 5 =$ ____

$5 + 0 =$ ____

$2 + 3 =$ ____

A Touch of Color

Name _____ Date _____

Add.
Color by the code.

Color Code

7—blue
8—orange
9—yellow
10—red

$$5 + 2$$

$$1 + 7$$

$$2 + 7$$

$$4 + 5$$

$$7 + 3$$

$$3 + 4$$

$$1 + 8$$

$$4 + 6$$

$$6 + 2$$

$$8 + 2$$

$$8 + 1$$

$$3 + 5$$

$$8 + 0$$

$$5 + 5$$

$$6 + 3$$

Them Bones

Name _____ Date _____

There are 206 bones in an adult body. But how many bones are in your body when you are born?

Add.
If the answer is **9** or **10**, color it **yellow**.

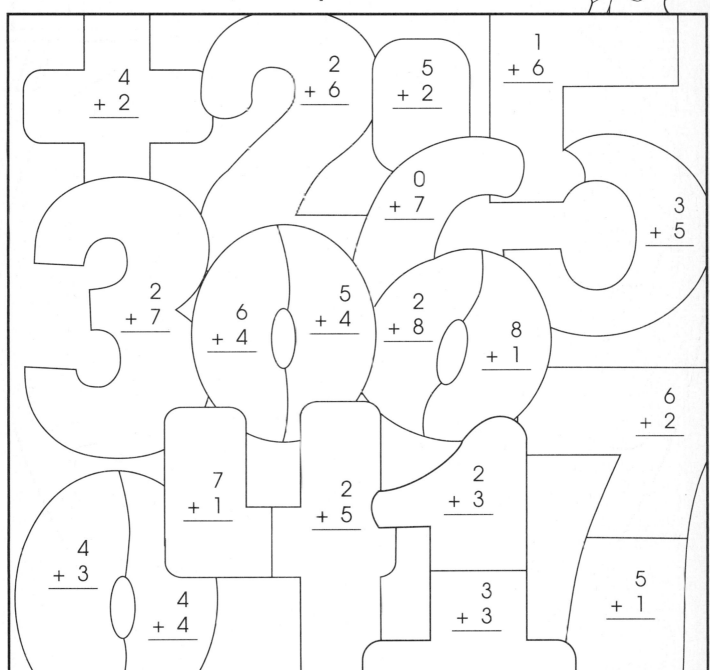

Here a Chick! Where a Chick?

Name _____ Date _____

Add.

Help Mother Hen find her chicks.

If the answer is **10**, color the bag **brown**.

$$\begin{array}{r} 2 \\ + 4 \\ \hline \end{array} \qquad \begin{array}{r} 6 \\ + 1 \\ \hline \end{array} \qquad \begin{array}{r} 3 \\ + 5 \\ \hline \end{array} \qquad \begin{array}{r} 0 \\ + 4 \\ \hline \end{array}$$

$$\begin{array}{r} 0 \\ + 10 \\ \hline \end{array} \qquad \begin{array}{r} 9 \\ + 1 \\ \hline \end{array} \qquad \begin{array}{r} 5 \\ + 5 \\ \hline \end{array} \qquad \begin{array}{r} 9 \\ + 0 \\ \hline \end{array} \qquad \begin{array}{r} 1 \\ + 4 \\ \hline \end{array}$$

$$\begin{array}{r} 4 \\ + 3 \\ \hline \end{array} \qquad \begin{array}{r} 2 \\ + 7 \\ \hline \end{array} \qquad \begin{array}{r} 6 \\ + 4 \\ \hline \end{array} \qquad \begin{array}{r} 5 \\ + 4 \\ \hline \end{array} \qquad \begin{array}{r} 3 \\ + 3 \\ \hline \end{array}$$

$$\begin{array}{r} 3 \\ + 2 \\ \hline \end{array} \qquad \begin{array}{r} 4 \\ + 4 \\ \hline \end{array} \qquad \begin{array}{r} 2 \\ + 8 \\ \hline \end{array} \qquad \begin{array}{r} 3 \\ + 7 \\ \hline \end{array} \qquad \begin{array}{r} 1 \\ + 9 \\ \hline \end{array}$$

$$\begin{array}{r} 2 \\ + 5 \\ \hline \end{array} \qquad \begin{array}{r} 4 \\ + 0 \\ \hline \end{array} \qquad \begin{array}{r} 6 \\ + 2 \\ \hline \end{array}$$

Hanging Out at the Castle

Name _____ Date _____

Read.
Write the math sentence.

Dragons are #1

There are 2 dragons.
7 more dragons come in.
How many dragons in all?

____ + ____ = ____

The castle has 1 front door.
It has 6 back doors.
How many doors in all?

____ + ____ = ____

The dragons have 6 pets.
They get 4 more.
How many pets in all?

____ + ____ = ____

The dragons eat 3 hot dots.
They eat 5 more.
How many hot dogs in all?

____ + ____ = ____

There are 3 flags.
There are 7 more.
How many flags
   in all?

____ + ____ = ____

5 dragons are green.
4 dragons are blue.
How many dragons
   in all?

____ + ____ = ____

Dragons
Welcome

Story problems: adding to 10

Schoolhouse Sums

Name _____ Date _____

Read.
Write the math sentence.

School

There are 4 boys.
There are 4 girls.
How many kids in all?

_____ + _____ = _____

The teacher has 2 apples. She gets 6 more. How many apples in all?	The bell rings 5 times. It rings 5 times more. How many rings in all?
_____ + _____ = _____	_____ + _____ = _____
The girls get 9 stickers. They get 1 more. How many stickers in all?	The boy has 6 markers. He gets 3 more. How many markers in all?
_____ + _____ = _____	_____ + _____ = _____
The class has 4 books. The class gets 6 more. How many books in all?	There are 8 desks. There is 1 more. How many desks in all?
_____ + _____ = _____	_____ + _____ = _____

Parrot's Treasure

Name ______________________________ Date ______________

Add.
Color by the code.

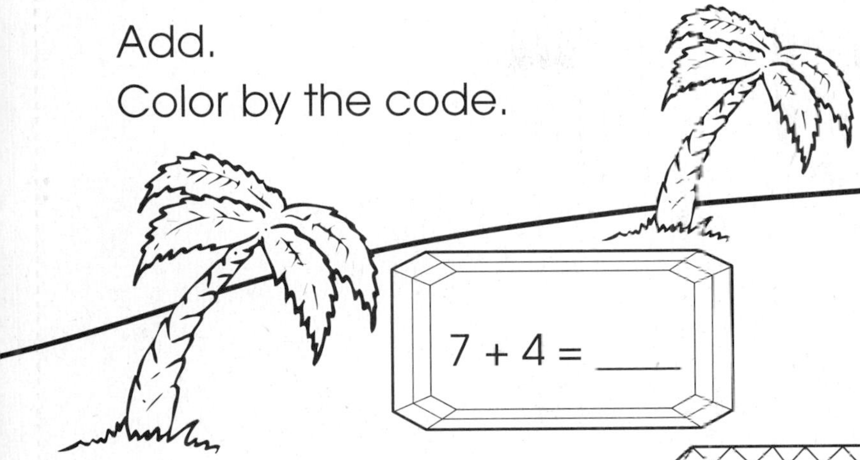

Color Code

8—red 10—blue
9—orange 11—purple

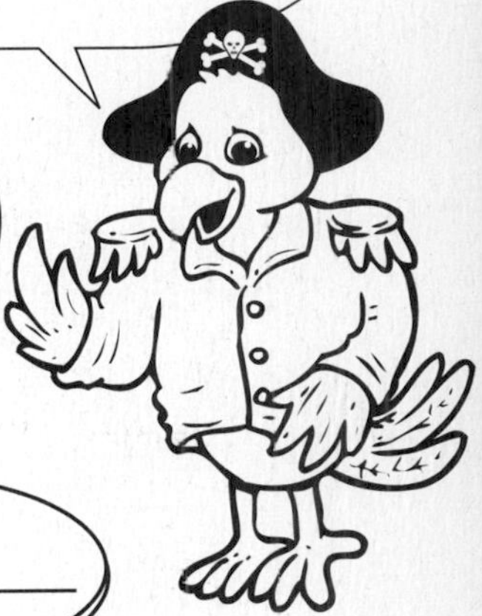

7 + 4 = ____

9 + 2 = ____

4 + 5 = ____

1 + 8 = ____

5 + 6 = ____

1 + 7 = ____

3 + 8 = ____

5 + 5 = ____

6 + 5 = ____

7 + 2 = ____

4 + 7 = ____

2 + 6 = ____

2 + 7 = ____

7 + 1 = ____

6 + 4 = ____

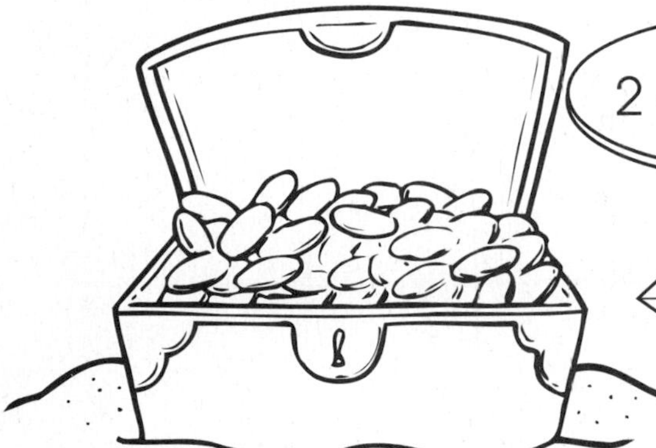

2 + 9 = ____

8 + 3 = ____

3 + 5 = ____

10 + 0 = ____

Hip-Hop Polar Pals

Name _____ Date _____

Add.
Match the letters to the numbered lines
below to solve the riddle.

What did the polar
bear say when he saw
his penguin friend?

4 + 5 **Y**	0 + 2 **C**	3 + 7 **L**	2 + 9 **D**	6 + 2 **R**
7 + 4 **D**	1 + 3 **E**	2 + 1 **O**	4 + 2 **U**	2 + 3 **A**
5 + 6 **D**	0 + 3 **O**	9 + 2 **D**	1 + 2 **O**	4 + 3 **S**
6 + 0 **U**	8 + 3 **D**	3 + 3 **U**	3 + 0 **O**	6 + 5 **D**

___ ___ ___   ___ ___ ___   ___ ___   ___ ___ ___ ___ !
 9   3   6   5   8   4   7   3   2   3   3   10

Chow Time!

Add.
Color by the code.

$$4 + 5$$

$$1 + 7 \qquad 4 + 4 \qquad 8 + 0 \qquad 5 + 3 \qquad 2 + 6 \qquad 7 + 1$$

$$8 + 1$$

$$2 + 8$$

$$0 + 8$$

$$5 + 4$$

$$4 + 6$$

$$8 + 3$$

$$9 + 2$$

$$3 + 5$$

$$7 + 3$$

$$9 + 1$$

$$6 + 2$$

$$6 + 5$$

$$7 + 2$$

$$9 + 0$$

$$3 + 8 \qquad 5 + 6 \qquad 4 + 7 \qquad 7 + 4 \qquad 2 + 9$$

$$0 + 9$$

$$2 + 7$$

Color Code
8—red   9—yellow   10 or 11—brown

©The Education Center, Inc. • *Target Math Success* • TEC60825 • Key p. 130

Par for the Course!

Name _____ Date _____

Add.

Gopher needs to find the next golf tee.

If the answer is **10** or **11,** color the box
brown to make a tunnel.

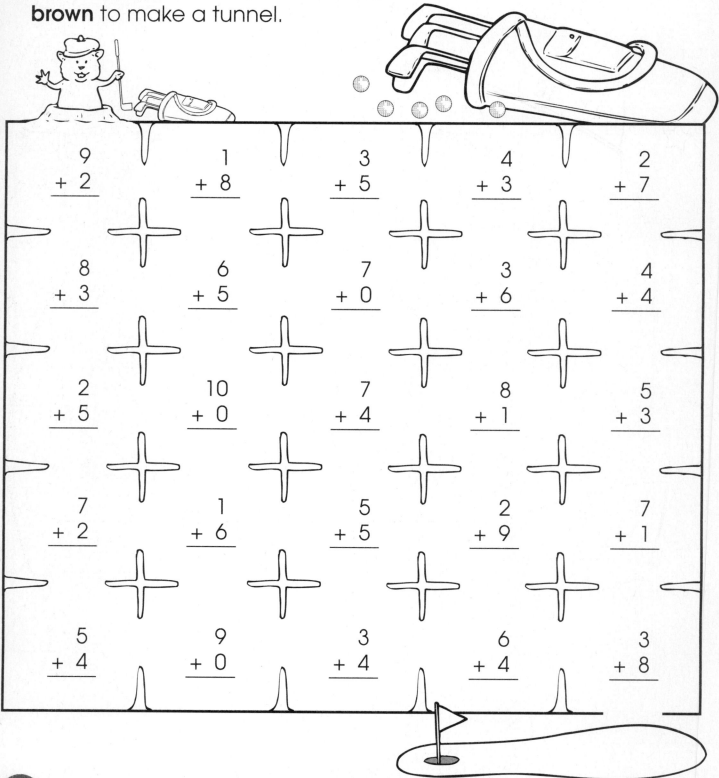

$$\begin{array}{r} 9 \\ + 2 \\ \hline \end{array} \quad \begin{array}{r} 1 \\ + 8 \\ \hline \end{array} \quad \begin{array}{r} 3 \\ + 5 \\ \hline \end{array} \quad \begin{array}{r} 4 \\ + 3 \\ \hline \end{array} \quad \begin{array}{r} 2 \\ + 7 \\ \hline \end{array}$$

$$\begin{array}{r} 8 \\ + 3 \\ \hline \end{array} \quad \begin{array}{r} 6 \\ + 5 \\ \hline \end{array} \quad \begin{array}{r} 7 \\ + 0 \\ \hline \end{array} \quad \begin{array}{r} 3 \\ + 6 \\ \hline \end{array} \quad \begin{array}{r} 4 \\ + 4 \\ \hline \end{array}$$

$$\begin{array}{r} 2 \\ + 5 \\ \hline \end{array} \quad \begin{array}{r} 10 \\ + 0 \\ \hline \end{array} \quad \begin{array}{r} 7 \\ + 4 \\ \hline \end{array} \quad \begin{array}{r} 8 \\ + 1 \\ \hline \end{array} \quad \begin{array}{r} 5 \\ + 3 \\ \hline \end{array}$$

$$\begin{array}{r} 7 \\ + 2 \\ \hline \end{array} \quad \begin{array}{r} 1 \\ + 6 \\ \hline \end{array} \quad \begin{array}{r} 5 \\ + 5 \\ \hline \end{array} \quad \begin{array}{r} 2 \\ + 9 \\ \hline \end{array} \quad \begin{array}{r} 7 \\ + 1 \\ \hline \end{array}$$

$$\begin{array}{r} 5 \\ + 4 \\ \hline \end{array} \quad \begin{array}{r} 9 \\ + 0 \\ \hline \end{array} \quad \begin{array}{r} 3 \\ + 4 \\ \hline \end{array} \quad \begin{array}{r} 6 \\ + 4 \\ \hline \end{array} \quad \begin{array}{r} 3 \\ + 8 \\ \hline \end{array}$$

Mouse on the Moon!

Name _____   Date _____

Add.
Cross out a matching answer.

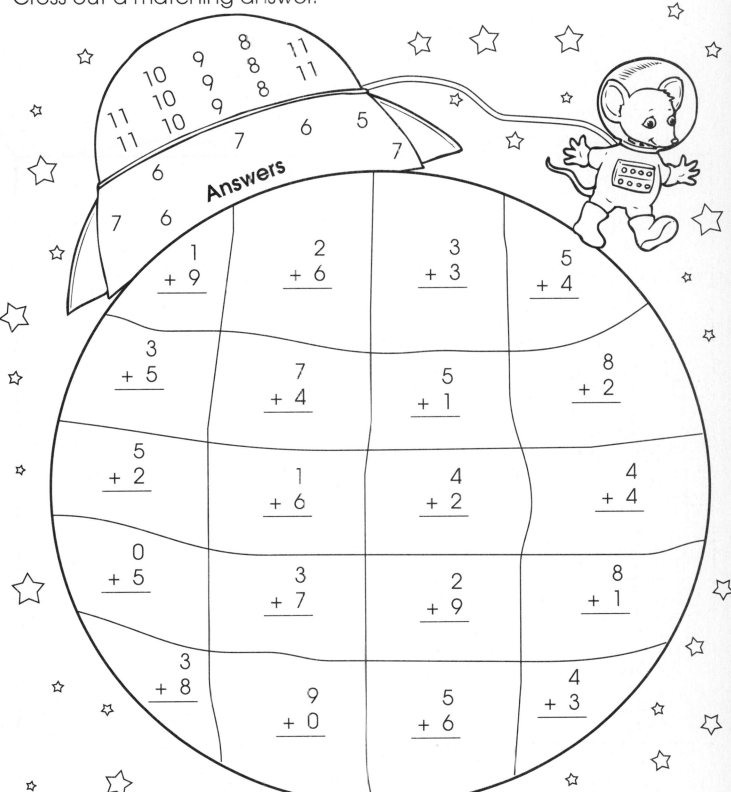

Answers

8 9 11
10 9 8 11
11 10 9 8 11
11 10 9 8
11 10 7 6 5
6 7
7 6

1 + 9	2 + 6	3 + 3	5 + 4
3 + 5	7 + 4	5 + 1	8 + 2
5 + 2	1 + 6	4 + 2	4 + 4
0 + 5	3 + 7	2 + 9	8 + 1
3 + 8	9 + 0	5 + 6	4 + 3

Catnap

Name _____ Date _____

Add.

1 + 9 = _____
9 + 1 = _____

3 + 8 = _____
8 + 3 = _____

4 + 6 = _____
6 + 4 = _____

9 + 2 = _____
2 + 9 = _____

4 + 7 = _____
7 + 4 = _____

10 + 0 = _____
0 + 10 = _____

3 + 7 = _____
7 + 3 = _____

5 + 6 = _____
6 + 5 = _____

2 + 8 = _____
8 + 2 = _____

54 **Turn-around facts: adding to 11**

Monkey Island

Name _____ Date _____

Add.
Color by the code.

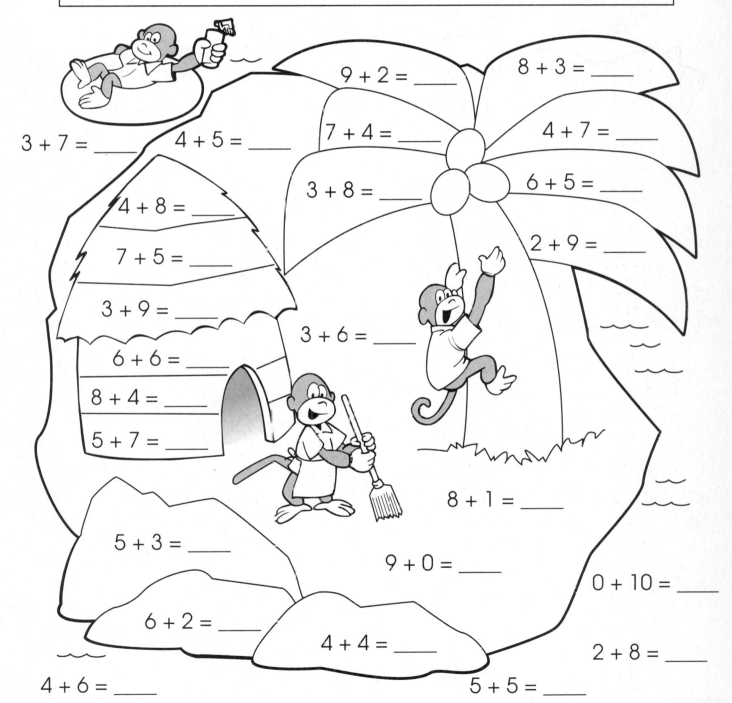

Color Code

8—black 9—brown 10—blue 11—green 12—yellow

9 + 2 = ____

8 + 3 = ____

3 + 7 = ____

4 + 5 = ____

7 + 4 = ____

4 + 7 = ____

3 + 8 = ____

6 + 5 = ____

4 + 8 = ____

7 + 5 = ____

3 + 9 = ____

2 + 9 = ____

6 + 6 = ____

8 + 4 = ____

3 + 6 = ____

5 + 7 = ____

8 + 1 = ____

5 + 3 = ____

9 + 0 = ____

0 + 10 = ____

6 + 2 = ____

4 + 4 = ____

2 + 8 = ____

4 + 6 = ____

5 + 5 = ____

Hopping Off to School

Name _____ Date _____

Add.

Help Joey get to school.

If the answer is **11** or **12**, color it **green**.

5 + 1	2 + 6	3 + 4

2 + 7	3 + 9	8 + 4	7 + 5	3 + 6
5 + 4	5 + 2	1 + 9	2 + 9	2 + 8
5 + 7	6 + 5	4 + 7	4 + 8	0 + 7
8 + 3	5 + 5	8 + 1	7 + 3	
9 + 3	6 + 6	5 + 6		

RING!
RING!

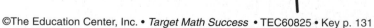

Dive Right In!

Name _____ Date _____

Add.

Cross off a matching answer.

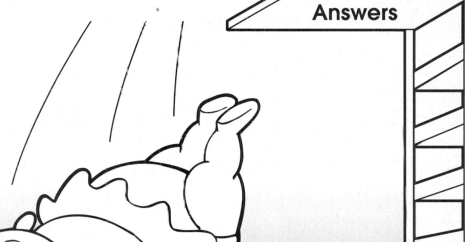

Answers

12
12
12
12
12
11
11
11
11
10
10
10
10
9
9
9

1 + 8	5 + 7	9 + 2	8 + 4	2 + 7

4 + 6	6 + 6	9 + 1	4 + 7	3 + 9

5 + 4	9 + 3	8 + 2	6 + 5	3 + 7	3 + 8

Riddle Roundup

Name _____ Date _____

Add.
Write the matching letters from the code.
Read the riddle answer.

When is it safe to run without tying your shoes?

Code
3 — y
4 — s
5 — u
6 — a
7 — w
8 — n
9 — h
10 — r
11 — o
12 — e

$\begin{array}{r} 5 \\ +2 \\ \hline \end{array}$ $\begin{array}{r} 2 \\ +7 \\ \hline \end{array}$ $\begin{array}{r} 8 \\ +4 \\ \hline \end{array}$ $\begin{array}{r} 3 \\ +5 \\ \hline \end{array}$

___ ___ ___ ___

$\begin{array}{r} 2 \\ +1 \\ \hline \end{array}$ $\begin{array}{r} 9 \\ +2 \\ \hline \end{array}$ $\begin{array}{r} 3 \\ +2 \\ \hline \end{array}$, $\begin{array}{r} 6 \\ +4 \\ \hline \end{array}$ $\begin{array}{r} 3 \\ +9 \\ \hline \end{array}$ $\begin{array}{r} 1 \\ +5 \\ \hline \end{array}$

___ ___ ___ , ___ ___ ___

$\begin{array}{r} 5 \\ +4 \\ \hline \end{array}$ $\begin{array}{r} 4 \\ +7 \\ \hline \end{array}$ $\begin{array}{r} 7 \\ +3 \\ \hline \end{array}$ $\begin{array}{r} 1 \\ +3 \\ \hline \end{array}$ $\begin{array}{r} 6 \\ +6 \\ \hline \end{array}$!

___ ___ ___ ___ ___ !

3...2...1... Blast Off

Name _____ Date _____

Write the math sentence.

U.S.A.

5 spaceships blast off. Then 2 more blast off. How many spaceships in all? ____ + ____ = ____	The spacehip makes 3 stops along the way. Then it makes 8 more. How many stops in all? ____ + ____ = ____
There are 6 dogs and 6 cats on the spaceship. How many animals in all? ____ + ____ = ____	They see 2 stars. Then they see 6 more. How many stars in all? ____ + ____ = ____
There are 7 big windows and 3 small windows. How many windows in all? ____ + ____ = ____	The dogs chew 8 bones. Then they chew 1 more. How many bones in all? ____ + ____ = ____

Race to the Finish Line

Name _____ Date _____

Write the math sentence.

Start Finish

There are 5 races. There are 5 more. How many races in all? ____ + ____ = ____	7 cars are in a race. 5 more cars race. How many cars in all? ____ + ____ = ____
They change 6 tires. They change 4 more. How many tires in all? ____ + ____ = ____	The cars make 4 laps. They make 8 more. How many laps in all? ____ + ____ = ____
They wave 6 flags. Then they wave 5 more. How many flags in all? ____ + ____ = ____	3 people are at the race. 9 more people come. How many people in all? ____ + ____ = ____
4 people fix the car. 7 more people help. How many people in all? ____ + ____ = ____	There are 6 red cars. There are 6 blue cars. How many cars in all? ____ + ____ = ____

Story problems: adding to 12

A Rain Forest Friend

Name _____   Date _____

Add.
Color by the code.

Color Code
7—brown   8—red   9—blue
10 or 11—green   12 or 13—black
14—white

$1 + 9 =$ _____

$8 + 5 =$ _____

$2 + 8 =$ _____

$6 + 2 =$ _____

$6 + 3 =$ _____

$9 + 2 =$ _____

$4 + 4 =$ _____

$5 + 9 =$ _____

$4 + 7 =$ _____

$7 + 7 =$ _____

$0 + 10 =$ _____

$8 + 2 =$ _____

$8 + 6 =$ _____

$4 + 9 =$ _____

$6 + 5 =$ _____

$5 + 7 =$ _____

$8 + 3 =$ _____

$2 + 9 =$ _____

$8 + 4 =$ _____

$6 + 7 =$ _____

$4 + 6 =$ _____

$3 + 7 =$ _____

$9 + 3 =$ _____

$6 + 1 =$ _____

Snail Mail

Name _____ Date _____

Add.

Help Snail deliver the mail.

If the answer is **12**, **13**, or **14**, color the box **green**.

6 + 8	6 + 7	9 + 4	8 + 6
7 + 4	3 + 8	1 + 9	2 + 7	4 + 9
5 + 4	9 + 3	7 + 7	6 + 6	8 + 5
3 + 6	5 + 8	9 + 1	6 + 4	7 + 3
8 + 2	9 + 5	7 + 6	4 + 8	3 + 9

The Slugmans

At the "Moo-vies"

Name _____ Date _____

Add.
Cross off a matching answer.

5 + 9	0 + 9	6 + 6	4 + 7	7 + 7	6 + 4
6 + 7	3 + 4	4 + 5	5 + 2	3 + 8	2 + 6
4 + 8	9 + 1	5 + 8	0 + 8	7 + 5	6 + 1
8 + 3	7 + 2	9 + 5	6 + 2	4 + 9	5 + 5

Answers

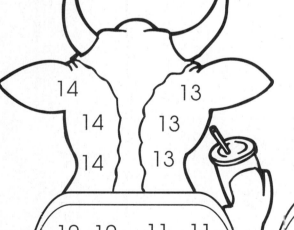

14   13
14   13
14   13

12 12 11 11
12   11

9
9
9

10
10
10

8   8   7 7
8   7

Send Me a Letter

Name _____ Date _____

Add.

Match the letters to the numbered lines below to solve the riddle.

What do you call two pigs that write each other letters?

4 + 9 L	8 + 6 P	5 + 4 G	6 + 2 O	2 + 8 S	7 + 7 P
7 + 3 S	9 + 5 P	3 + 9 I	5 + 5 S	9 + 0 G	4 + 7 A
2 + 9 A	5 + 3 O	10 + 0 S	4 + 4 O	8 + 3 A	6 + 3 G
6 + 6 I	6 + 4 S	5 + 9 P	4 + 8 I	6 + 8 P	4 + 6 S

___ ___ ___ ___ ___ ___ ___ ___!
14 12 9   14 11 13 10

Sweet Dreams!

Name _____   Date _____

Add.

Color by the code.

$$\begin{array}{r} 8 \\ + 6 \\ \hline \end{array}$$

$$\begin{array}{r} 7 \\ + 4 \\ \hline \end{array}$$

$$\begin{array}{r} 3 \\ + 9 \\ \hline \end{array}$$

$$\begin{array}{r} 9 \\ + 2 \\ \hline \end{array}$$

$$\begin{array}{r} 6 \\ + 6 \\ \hline \end{array}$$

$$\begin{array}{r} 5 \\ + 8 \\ \hline \end{array}$$

$$\begin{array}{r} 5 \\ + 7 \\ \hline \end{array}$$

$$\begin{array}{r} 7 \\ + 6 \\ \hline \end{array}$$

$$\begin{array}{r} 4 \\ + 9 \\ \hline \end{array}$$

$$\begin{array}{r} 5 \\ + 6 \\ \hline \end{array}$$

$$\begin{array}{r} 6 \\ + 8 \\ \hline \end{array}$$

$$\begin{array}{r} 7 \\ + 7 \\ \hline \end{array}$$

$$\begin{array}{r} 8 \\ + 3 \\ \hline \end{array}$$

$$\begin{array}{r} 8 \\ + 5 \\ \hline \end{array}$$

$$\begin{array}{r} 6 \\ + 7 \\ \hline \end{array}$$

$$\begin{array}{r} 4 \\ + 8 \\ \hline \end{array}$$

$$\begin{array}{r} 9 \\ + 4 \\ \hline \end{array}$$

$$\begin{array}{r} 7 \\ + 5 \\ \hline \end{array}$$

$$\begin{array}{r} 6 \\ + 5 \\ \hline \end{array}$$

$$\begin{array}{r} 7 \\ + 4 \\ \hline \end{array}$$

$$\begin{array}{r} 9 \\ + 3 \\ \hline \end{array}$$

$$\begin{array}{r} 5 \\ + 9 \\ \hline \end{array}$$

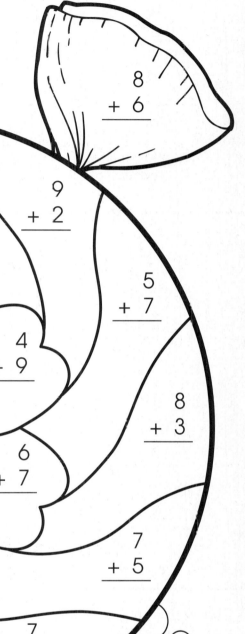

Color Code
11—green
12—purple
13—red
14—yellow

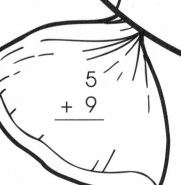

The One That Got Away!

Name _____   Date _____

Add.

5 + 9 = _____

9 + 5 = _____

6 + 7 = _____

7 + 6 = _____

4 + 7 = _____

7 + 4 = _____

3 + 9 = _____

9 + 3 = _____

3 + 8 = _____

8 + 3 = _____

5 + 6 = _____

6 + 5 = _____

4 + 9 = _____

9 + 4 = _____

6 + 8 = _____

8 + 6 = _____

8 + 5 = _____

5 + 8 = _____

7 + 5 = _____

5 + 7 = _____

4 + 8 = _____

8 + 4 = _____

2 + 9 = _____

9 + 2 = _____

Turn-around facts: adding to 14

This Takes the Cake!

Name _____ Date _____

Read each big number.
Circle 4 ways to make that number.

13

4 + 9
3 + 8
7 + 6
8 + 5
6 + 6
9 + 4

14

4 + 8
7 + 7
8 + 6
9 + 3
5 + 9
6 + 8

15

6 + 9
7 + 5
8 + 7
8 + 4
9 + 6
7 + 8

16

7 + 9
8 + 3
8 + 8
7 + 4
9 + 7
16 + 0

High-Flying Facts

Name _____ Date _____

Add.
Cross off a matching answer.

12	12	13	13	13	13	14	14
14	14	15	15	15	16	16	16

$$\begin{array}{cc} 5 \\ +9 \\ \hline \end{array} \quad \begin{array}{cc} 7 \\ +9 \\ \hline \end{array} \quad \begin{array}{cc} 8 \\ +5 \\ \hline \end{array} \quad \begin{array}{cc} 6 \\ +7 \\ \hline \end{array} \quad \begin{array}{cc} 4 \\ +8 \\ \hline \end{array} \quad \begin{array}{cc} 3 \\ +9 \\ \hline \end{array} \quad \begin{array}{cc} 9 \\ +7 \\ \hline \end{array} \quad \begin{array}{cc} 8 \\ +7 \\ \hline \end{array}$$

$$\begin{array}{cc} 6 \\ +9 \\ \hline \end{array} \quad \begin{array}{cc} 7 \\ +7 \\ \hline \end{array} \quad \begin{array}{cc} 4 \\ +9 \\ \hline \end{array} \quad \begin{array}{cc} 8 \\ +6 \\ \hline \end{array} \quad \begin{array}{cc} 8 \\ +8 \\ \hline \end{array} \quad \begin{array}{cc} 7 \\ +6 \\ \hline \end{array} \quad \begin{array}{cc} 9 \\ +5 \\ \hline \end{array} \quad \begin{array}{cc} 7 \\ +8 \\ \hline \end{array}$$

And the Winner Is...

Name _____ Date _____

Add.
Color by the code.

FINISH

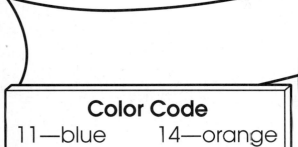

Color Code

11—blue	14—orange
12—red	15—green
13—purple	16—yellow

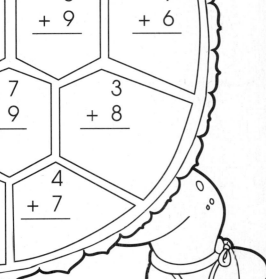

$$6 + 7$$

$$8 + 8$$

$$6 + 9$$

$$7 + 8$$

$$5 + 9$$

$$4 + 9$$

$$4 + 8$$

$$9 + 7$$

$$7 + 7$$

$$2 + 9$$

$$3 + 9$$

$$9 + 6$$

$$5 + 8$$

$$8 + 7$$

$$7 + 9$$

$$3 + 8$$

$$6 + 8$$

$$5 + 7$$

$$4 + 7$$

Dressed and Ready to Go!

Name _____ Date _____

Add.
Color by the code.

$$\begin{array}{r} 7 \\ +\ 9 \\ \hline \end{array}$$

$$\begin{array}{r} 6 \\ +\ 8 \\ \hline \end{array}$$

$$\begin{array}{r} 9 \\ +\ 4 \\ \hline \end{array}$$

$$\begin{array}{r} 4 \\ +\ 8 \\ \hline \end{array}$$

$$\begin{array}{r} 5 \\ +\ 8 \\ \hline \end{array}$$

$$\begin{array}{r} 8 \\ +\ 8 \\ \hline \end{array}$$

$$\begin{array}{r} 5 \\ +\ 7 \\ \hline \end{array}$$

$$\begin{array}{r} 6 \\ +\ 7 \\ \hline \end{array}$$

$$\begin{array}{r} 7 \\ +\ 8 \\ \hline \end{array}$$

$$\begin{array}{r} 7 \\ +\ 7 \\ \hline \end{array}$$

$$\begin{array}{r} 9 \\ +\ 5 \\ \hline \end{array}$$

$$\begin{array}{r} 9 \\ +\ 7 \\ \hline \end{array}$$

$$\begin{array}{r} 8 \\ +\ 4 \\ \hline \end{array}$$

$$\begin{array}{r} 7 \\ +\ 5 \\ \hline \end{array}$$

$$\begin{array}{r} 6 \\ +\ 9 \\ \hline \end{array}$$

$$\begin{array}{r} 9 \\ +\ 6 \\ \hline \end{array}$$

$$\begin{array}{r} 8 \\ +\ 5 \\ \hline \end{array}$$

$$\begin{array}{r} 7 \\ +\ 6 \\ \hline \end{array}$$

$$\begin{array}{r} 4 \\ +\ 9 \\ \hline \end{array}$$

Dino Drive-In

Name _____ Date _____

Write the math sentence.

8 cars are at the movie. 8 more come. How many cars in all? _____ + _____ = _____	The dinosaur eats 6 hot dogs. He eats 9 more. How many hot dogs in all? _____ + _____ = _____
7 dinosaurs are in a car. 9 more dinosaurs join them. How many dinosaurs in all? _____ + _____ = _____	9 cars are white. 5 cars are black. How many cars in all? _____ + _____ = _____
The dinosaurs watch 6 movies. They watch 8 more movies. How many movies in all? _____ + _____ = _____	The dinosaur buys 8 drinks. He buys 7 more drinks. How many drinks in all? _____ + _____ = _____

Story problems: adding to 16

Choo! Choo!

Name _____ Date _____

Write the math sentence.

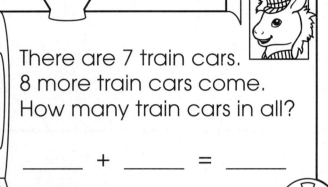

There are 7 train cars.
8 more train cars come.
How many train cars in all?

_____ + _____ = _____

The train drives 6 miles.
It drives 9 more miles.
How many miles in all?

_____ + _____ = _____

7 horses are on the train.
7 more horses come.
How many horses in all?

_____ + _____ = _____

There are 7 boxcars.
There are 9 more boxcars.
How many boxcars in all?

_____ + _____ = _____

The horses ride for 6 days.
They ride for 8 more days.
How many days in all?

_____ + _____ = _____

The horse rings the bell 8
   times.
Then he rings it 8 more times.
How many rings in all?

_____ + _____ = _____

That's "Bear-y" Funny!

Name _____   Date _____

Add.
Write the matching letters from the code.
Read the riddle answer.

 What do you call a bear with no shoes?

6 + 8 = ____ R	9 + 6 = ____ E	8 + 8 = ____ O	6 + 7 = ____ B
5 + 9 = ____ R	7 + 8 = ____ E	9 + 4 = ____ B	9 + 9 = ____ A
4 + 8 = ____ F	7 + 9 = ____ O	8 + 7 = ____ E	8 + 4 = ____ F
8 + 9 = ____ T	7 + 7 = ____ R	6 + 6 = ____ F	4 + 9 = ____ B
8 + 5 = ____ B	6 + 9 = ____ E	8 + 6 = ____ R	9 + 7 = ____ O
7 + 6 = ____ B	9 + 8 = ____ T	9 + 5 = ____ R	5 + 8 = ____ B

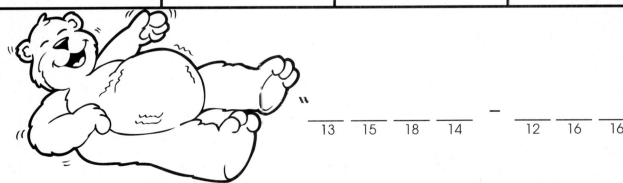

" ___ ___ ___ ___ – ___ ___ ___ ___ "
  13 15 18 14   12 16 16 17

Hurry On Home!

Name _____   Date _____

Add.

Help Raccoon get home for dinner.

If the answer is **16, 17,** or **18,** color the box **brown.**

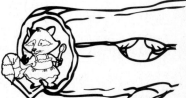

Home

8 + 5	7 + 8	5 + 9	9 + 3	9 + 8
6 + 9	7 + 7	5 + 8	6 + 7	9 + 7
4 + 9	8 + 6	9 + 4	8 + 8	7 + 10
7 + 9	10 + 8	8 + 9	6 + 10	6 + 9

Start

Stay on the path!

Really! It's True!

Name _____   Date _____

Read.
Add.
Color by the code.

How many stomachs does a cow have?

7 + 9	8 + 7	5 + 9	7 + 7	9 + 6	8 + 9
4 + 8	2 + 9	9 + 4	5 + 5	5 + 7	7 + 6
6 + 6	8 + 3	4 + 7	8 + 2	6 + 6	3 + 9
9 + 9	8 + 6	6 + 9	1 + 9	9 + 5	9 + 8

Hungry Little Rabbit!

Name _____   Date _____

Read.
Add.
Color by the code.

$$\begin{array}{r} 9 \\ + 7 \\ \hline \end{array}$$

$$\begin{array}{r} 6 \\ + 6 \\ \hline \end{array}$$

$$\begin{array}{r} 3 \\ + 8 \\ \hline \end{array}$$

$$\begin{array}{r} 5 \\ + 6 \\ \hline \end{array}$$

$$\begin{array}{r} 7 \\ + 8 \\ \hline \end{array}$$

$$\begin{array}{r} 8 \\ + 9 \\ \hline \end{array}$$

Color Code
11—yellow
12, 13, or 14—green
15—orange
16—red
17 or 18—brown

$$\begin{array}{r} 6 \\ + 7 \\ \hline \end{array}$$

$$\begin{array}{r} 9 \\ + 8 \\ \hline \end{array}$$

$$\begin{array}{r} 8 \\ + 4 \\ \hline \end{array}$$

$$\begin{array}{r} 9 \\ + 4 \\ \hline \end{array}$$

$$\begin{array}{r} 7 \\ + 5 \\ \hline \end{array}$$

$$\begin{array}{r} 6 \\ + 9 \\ \hline \end{array}$$

$$\begin{array}{r} 9 \\ + 3 \\ \hline \end{array}$$

$$\begin{array}{r} 7 \\ + 6 \\ \hline \end{array}$$

$$\begin{array}{r} 6 \\ + 8 \\ \hline \end{array}$$

$$\begin{array}{r} 9 \\ + 9 \\ \hline \end{array}$$

$$\begin{array}{r} 5 \\ + 9 \\ \hline \end{array}$$

$$\begin{array}{r} 7 \\ + 9 \\ \hline \end{array}$$

$$\begin{array}{r} 7 \\ + 7 \\ \hline \end{array}$$

$$\begin{array}{r} 3 \\ + 9 \\ \hline \end{array}$$

$$\begin{array}{r} 8 \\ + 8 \\ \hline \end{array}$$

$$\begin{array}{r} 5 \\ + 7 \\ \hline \end{array}$$

$$\begin{array}{r} 4 \\ + 9 \\ \hline \end{array}$$

$$\begin{array}{r} 8 \\ + 7 \\ \hline \end{array}$$

Adding to 18

Yum! Cookies and Milk

Name _____ Date _____

Add.

Cross out the matching answer.

12 15 14 16 13

6 + 6 = _____

4 + 9 = _____

5 + 9 = _____

7 + 8 = _____

7 + 9 = _____

18 15 13 14 15

8 + 7 = _____

9 + 9 = _____

6 + 9 = _____

7 + 7 = _____

8 + 5 = _____

17 15 14 13 16

9 + 8 = _____

9 + 6 = _____

8 + 8 = _____

5 + 8 = _____

9 + 5 = _____

16 14 17 13 14

8 + 6 = _____

9 + 7 = _____

6 + 8 = _____

8 + 9 = _____

9 + 4 = _____

C n I Ride in th Buggy?

Name _____ Date _____

Read.
Write the math sentence.

Baby wants 6 fish. Baby wants 6 more fish. How many fish in all? _____ + _____ = _____	Mom chooses 2 donuts. She chooses 9 more donuts. How many donuts in all? _____ + _____ = _____
Mom needs 8 muffins. She needs 8 more muffins. How many muffins in all? _____ + _____ = _____	Baby eats 9 grapes. Baby eats 9 more grapes. How many grapes in all? _____ + _____ = _____
Baby picks out 9 juices. Baby picks out 8 more juices. How many juices in all? _____ + _____ = _____	Mom wants 7 apples. She wants 8 more apples. How many apples in all? _____ + _____ = _____

Story problems: adding to 18

Column Addition

Column Addition

Table of Contents

Strike!

Name _____ Date _____

Add.

Color by the code.

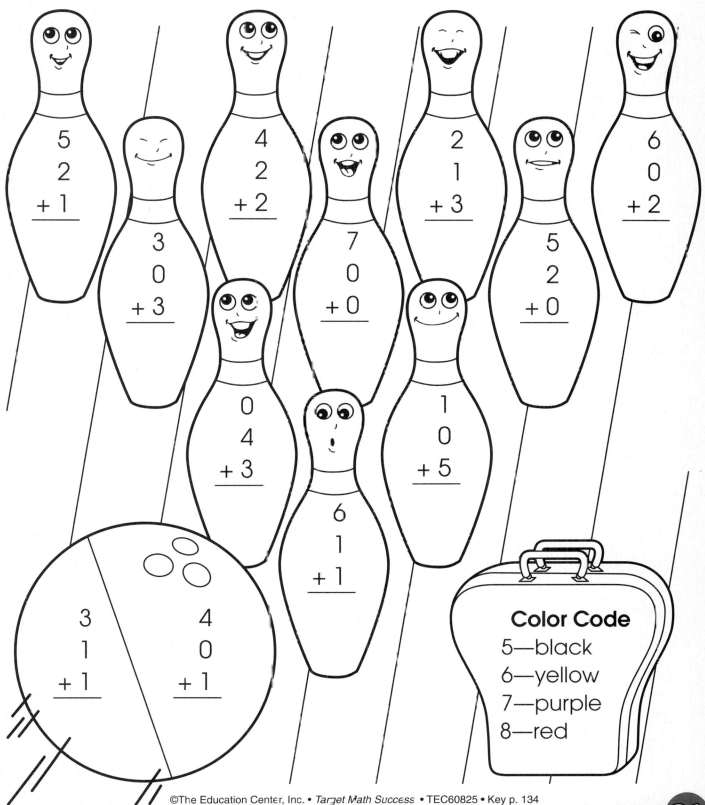

$$\begin{array}{r} 5 \\ 2 \\ +1 \\ \hline \end{array}$$

$$\begin{array}{r} 3 \\ 0 \\ +3 \\ \hline \end{array}$$

$$\begin{array}{r} 4 \\ 2 \\ +2 \\ \hline \end{array}$$

$$\begin{array}{r} 7 \\ 0 \\ +0 \\ \hline \end{array}$$

$$\begin{array}{r} 2 \\ 1 \\ +3 \\ \hline \end{array}$$

$$\begin{array}{r} 5 \\ 2 \\ +0 \\ \hline \end{array}$$

$$\begin{array}{r} 6 \\ 0 \\ +2 \\ \hline \end{array}$$

$$\begin{array}{r} 0 \\ 4 \\ +3 \\ \hline \end{array}$$

$$\begin{array}{r} 1 \\ 0 \\ +5 \\ \hline \end{array}$$

$$\begin{array}{r} 6 \\ 1 \\ +1 \\ \hline \end{array}$$

$$\begin{array}{r} 3 \\ 1 \\ +1 \\ \hline \end{array}$$

$$\begin{array}{r} 4 \\ 0 \\ +1 \\ \hline \end{array}$$

Color Code
5—black
6—yellow
7—purple
8—red

Column addition to 8 81

Musical Mouse Melody

Name _____ Date _____

Add.
Color by the code.

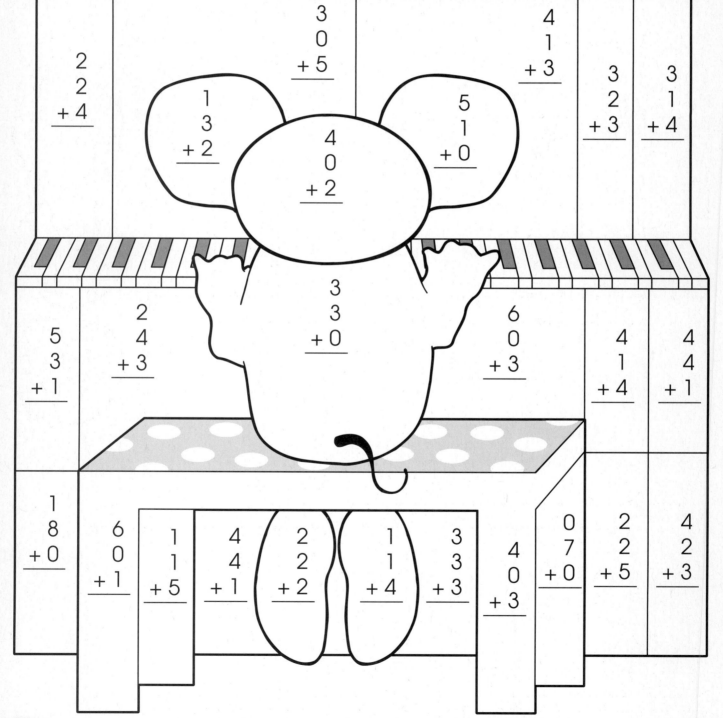

A Froggy Wedding

Name _____ Date _____

Add.
Write the matching letters from the code.
Read the riddle answer.

What do frogs do after they get married?

Code

1 — a
2 — i
3 — v

4 — h
5 — y

6 — p
7 — r
8 — t

9 — l
10—e

$$
\begin{array}{cccc}
4 & 3 & 5 & 2 \\
3 & 1 & 4 & 1 \\
+1 & +0 & +1 & +2 \\
\hline
\end{array}
\qquad
\begin{array}{cccc}
1 & 1 & 1 & 7 \\
4 & 1 & 2 & 3 \\
+4 & +0 & +0 & +0 \\
\hline
\end{array}
$$

$$
\begin{array}{ccccccc}
2 & & 3 & 1 & 2 & 2 & 5 \\
1 & & 2 & 4 & 0 & 5 & 0 \\
+1 & & +1 & +1 & +0 & +2 & +0 \\
\hline
 & 0 & & & & & \\
\end{array}
$$

$$
\begin{array}{cccc}
6 & 3 & 9 & 2 \\
2 & 0 & 0 & 1 \\
+2 & +0 & +1 & +4 \\
\hline
\end{array}
\qquad
\begin{array}{ccccc}
0 & & 6 & 3 & 4 \\
0 & & 2 & 3 & 3 \\
+1 & & +0 & +4 & +0 \\
\hline
f & & & & \\
\end{array}
$$

Just Hanging Around

Name _____ Date _____

Add.
Color by the code.

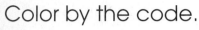

```
  5      4      2      4      7      8      3
  5      4      7      3      3      1      3
+ 1    + 2    + 0    + 1    + 1    + 0    + 4
```

```
  6      4      6      6      3      6      2
  4      1      1      3      3      3      4
+ 1    + 5    + 1    + 2    + 3    + 1    + 2
```

```
  2      4      4      2      9      5
  6      4      4      5      2      2
+ 2    + 3    + 1    + 3    + 0    + 1
```

Color Code
8—purple 10—green
9—blue   11—red

A Wild Ride!

Name _____ Date _____

Add.
Ride the roller coaster.
If the answer is **11** or **12**, color the track.

The Panther Blaster

$$\begin{array}{r} 5 \\ 7 \\ + \ 0 \\ \hline \end{array}$$

$$\begin{array}{r} 5 \\ 2 \\ + \ 1 \\ \hline \end{array}$$

$$\begin{array}{r} 3 \\ 2 \\ + \ 1 \\ \hline \end{array}$$

$$\begin{array}{r} 4 \\ 4 \\ + \ 3 \\ \hline \end{array}$$

$$\begin{array}{r} 4 \\ 3 \\ + \ 1 \\ \hline \end{array}$$

$$\begin{array}{r} 5 \\ 4 \\ + \ 2 \\ \hline \end{array}$$

$$\begin{array}{r} 5 \\ 2 \\ + \ 0 \\ \hline \end{array}$$

$$\begin{array}{r} 6 \\ 5 \\ + \ 1 \\ \hline \end{array}$$

$$\begin{array}{r} 6 \\ 1 \\ + \ 1 \\ \hline \end{array}$$

$$\begin{array}{r} 8 \\ 2 \\ + \ 1 \\ \hline \end{array}$$

$$\begin{array}{r} 8 \\ 3 \\ + \ 0 \\ \hline \end{array}$$

$$\begin{array}{r} 4 \\ 3 \\ + \ 5 \\ \hline \end{array}$$

$$\begin{array}{r} 6 \\ 4 \\ + \ 1 \\ \hline \end{array}$$

$$\begin{array}{r} 2 \\ 7 \\ + \ 2 \\ \hline \end{array}$$

$$\begin{array}{r} 7 \\ 4 \\ + \ 1 \\ \hline \end{array}$$

$$\begin{array}{r} 9 \\ 3 \\ + \ 0 \\ \hline \end{array}$$

$$\begin{array}{r} 2 \\ 4 \\ + \ 3 \\ \hline \end{array}$$

The End

High-Flying Numbers

Name _____ Date _____

Add.
Color a matching answer.

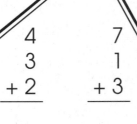

$$
\begin{array}{r} 4 \\ 3 \\ +2 \\ \hline \end{array}
\qquad
\begin{array}{r} 7 \\ 1 \\ +3 \\ \hline \end{array}
$$

$$
\begin{array}{r} 5 \\ 2 \\ +4 \\ \hline \end{array}
\quad
\begin{array}{r} 6 \\ 3 \\ +1 \\ \hline \end{array}
\quad
\begin{array}{r} 7 \\ 2 \\ +0 \\ \hline \end{array}
\quad
\begin{array}{r} 5 \\ 2 \\ +7 \\ \hline \end{array}
\quad
\begin{array}{r} 4 \\ 5 \\ +4 \\ \hline \end{array}
$$

$$
\begin{array}{r} 8 \\ 3 \\ +3 \\ \hline \end{array}
\quad
\begin{array}{r} 7 \\ 3 \\ +4 \\ \hline \end{array}
\quad
\begin{array}{r} 0 \\ 6 \\ +7 \\ \hline \end{array}
\quad
\begin{array}{r} 2 \\ 5 \\ +7 \\ \hline \end{array}
\quad
\begin{array}{r} 3 \\ 5 \\ +4 \\ \hline \end{array}
$$

$$
\begin{array}{r} 2 \\ 9 \\ +3 \\ \hline \end{array}
\quad
\begin{array}{r} 3 \\ 6 \\ +3 \\ \hline \end{array}
\quad
\begin{array}{r} 8 \\ 4 \\ +1 \\ \hline \end{array}
\quad
\begin{array}{r} 2 \\ 6 \\ +4 \\ \hline \end{array}
$$

$$
\begin{array}{r} 3 \\ 2 \\ +8 \\ \hline \end{array}
\qquad
\begin{array}{r} 3 \\ 7 \\ +0 \\ \hline \end{array}
$$

Column addition to 14

Dinosaur Ditty

Name _____ Date _____

Add.
Color by the code.

A Music l Mummy Myst ry

Name _____ Date _____

Add.

If the answer is **18**, color it **red**.

What is a mummy's
favorite kind of music?

```
  6        2        6        4              2    6
  4        1        3        8         7    3    6
 +3       +7       +6       +3        4   +9   +2
                                     +5

  5        7        6        9         4         6
  5        7        4        8         5         5
 +8       +4       +8       +1        +9        +7

                             2
  9        6             4   9                 3       5
  9    7   2        4    8   0        7    3   9       9
  4    1  +4       8    +4  +0        1   +6  +6      +1
 +4   +8          +4                 +6
```

Addition Strategies

Addition Strategies

Table of Contents

Lookin' Good!

Name _____   Date _____

Add.

Match the letters to the numbered
  lines below to solve the riddle.

What do you call
a girl cow?

___ ___ ___ ___ ___ ___ ___ ___!
 7   15   12   5   9   16   4   18

2 + 1 **T**	5 + 1 **B**	7 + 1 **N**	9 + 1 **P**
3 + 1 **R**	4 + 1 **W**	6 + 1 **A**	8 + 1 **G**
11 + 1 **O**	14 + 1 **C**	16 + 1 **F**	12 + 1 **H**
13 + 1 **S**	15 + 1 **I**	17 + 1 **L**	10 + 1 **Z**

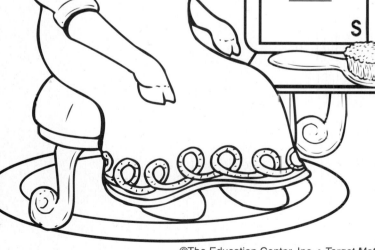

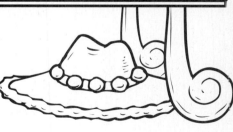

Oh, Good! The Math Channel!

Name _____ Date _____

Add.
Color the matching answer.

1 + 2	3 + 2	5 + 2	7 + 2
2 + 2	4 + 2	6 + 2	8 + 2
9 + 2	11 + 2	13 + 2	15 + 2
10 + 2	12 + 2	14 + 2	16 + 2

©The Education Center, Inc. • *Target Math Success* • TEC60825 • Key p. 135

Crunch, Crunch, Crunch

Name _____ Date _____

Add.

1 + 0	4 + 0	7 + 0	10 + 0	3 + 0	6 + 0
2 + 0	5 + 0	8 + 0	9 + 0	12 + 0	14 + 0
11 + 0	13 + 0	16 + 0	18 + 0	15 + 0	17 + 0

Make Mine a Double!

Name _____ Date _____

Add.
Color each ice cream by the
  code.

Color Code

2—pink   8—purple
4—green   10—brown
6—orange   12—yellow

$$\begin{array}{r}2\\+\ 2\\\hline\end{array}$$

$$\begin{array}{r}5\\+\ 5\\\hline\end{array}$$

$$\begin{array}{r}4\\+\ 4\\\hline\end{array}$$

$$\begin{array}{r}1\\+\ 1\\\hline\end{array}$$

$$\begin{array}{r}3\\+\ 3\\\hline\end{array}$$

$$\begin{array}{r}6\\+\ 6\\\hline\end{array}$$

$$\begin{array}{r}1\\+\ 1\\\hline\end{array}$$

$$\begin{array}{r}2\\+\ 2\\\hline\end{array}$$

$$\begin{array}{r}6\\+\ 6\\\hline\end{array}$$

$$\begin{array}{r}4\\+\ 4\\\hline\end{array}$$

$$\begin{array}{r}5\\+\ 5\\\hline\end{array}$$

$$\begin{array}{r}3\\+\ 3\\\hline\end{array}$$

Double Trouble

Name _____ Date _____

Add.

Circle each answer in the picture.

2 + 2 = ____

7 + 7 = ____

5 + 5 = ____

1 + 1 = ____

9 + 9 = ____

6 + 6 = ____

4 + 4 = ____

8 + 8 = ____

3 + 3 = ____

It's a Luau!

Name _____ Date _____

Add.

$$\begin{array}{r} 3 \\ + 4 \\ \hline \end{array}$$

$$\begin{array}{r} 2 \\ + 3 \\ \hline \end{array}$$

$$\begin{array}{r} 4 \\ + 5 \\ \hline \end{array}$$

$$\begin{array}{r} 1 \\ + 2 \\ \hline \end{array}$$

$$\begin{array}{r} 5 \\ + 6 \\ \hline \end{array}$$

$$\begin{array}{r} 6 \\ + 7 \\ \hline \end{array}$$

All Lights Aglow!

Name _____   Date _____

Add.

Doubles	Doubles + 1
2 + 2 = ____	2 + 3 = ____
6 + 6 = ____	6 + 7 = ____
3 + 3 = ____	3 + 4 = ____
8 + 8 = ____	8 + 9 = ____
4 + 4 = ____	4 + 5 = ____
1 + 1 = ____	1 + 2 = ____
7 + 7 = ____	7 + 8 = ____
5 + 5 = ____	5 + 6 = ____

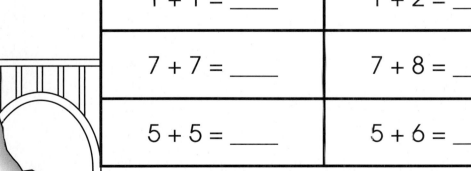

Doubles, doubles plus 1   97

Under the Big Top

Name _____ Date _____

Add.

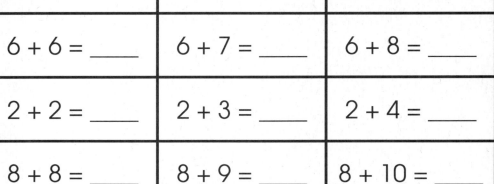

Doubles	Doubles + 1	Doubles + 2
3 + 3 = ____	3 + 4 = ____	3 + 5 = ____
5 + 5 = ____	5 + 6 = ____	5 + 7 = ____
7 + 7 = ____	7 + 8 = ____	7 + 9 = ____
1 + 1 = ____	1 + 2 = ____	1 + 3 = ____
4 + 4 = ____	4 + 5 = ____	4 + 6 = ____
6 + 6 = ____	6 + 7 = ____	6 + 8 = ____
2 + 2 = ____	2 + 3 = ____	2 + 4 = ____
8 + 8 = ____	8 + 9 = ____	8 + 10 = ____

©The Education Center, Inc. • Target Math Success • TEC60825 • Key p. 135

Doubles, doubles plus 1 and 2

Parent Communication and Student Checkups

Parent Communication and Student Checkups

Table of Contents

How to Administer the Checkups

Both checkups can be given at the same time, or Checkup B can be given as a follow-up test for students who did not do well on Checkup A. If desired, a time limit of **one minute** can be used when a test is given. This will help you determine which students have mastered a skill and which students may need more practice.

Student Progress Chart

(student)		Date	Number Correct	Comments
Checkup 1: Adding to Five	A			
	B			
Checkup 2: Adding to Six	A			
	B			
Checkup 3: Adding to Seven	A			
	B			
Checkup 4: Adding to Eight	A			
	B			
Checkup 5: Adding to Nine	A			
	B			
Checkup 6: Adding to Ten	A			
	B			
Checkup 7: Adding to Eleven	A			
	B			
Checkup 8: Adding to Twelve	A			
	B			
Checkup 9: Adding to Fourteen	A			
	B			
Checkup 10: Adding to Sixteen	A			
	B			
Checkup 11: Adding to Eighteen	A			
	B			

It's Time to Take Aim!

On _____ our class will be having a checkup on math facts. To help your child prepare, please spend about 15 minutes practicing math problems that review **adding to 5.** Thanks for your help!

Target These!

1	2
0 + 1	0 + 2
1 + 0	1 + 1
	2 + 0

4	3
0 + 4	0 + 3
1 + 3	1 + 2
2 + 2	2 + 1
3 + 1	3 + 0
4 + 0	

5

0 + 5
1 + 4
2 + 3
3 + 2
4 + 1
5 + 0

On-Target Practice

What do a coat hanger, five clothespins, and a piece of masking tape add up to? A handy math cure! Use the tape to mark the middle of the coat hanger as shown. Ask your child to attach three clothespins to the left of the tape and two to the right of the tape. Then have him say the math fact the clothespins represent *(3 + 2 = 5)*. After confirming his answer, have him remove the clothespins. Repeat this activity several more times, using five, four, three, two, one, or zero clothespins!

Wrap up by calling out the math problems at the right and having your child supply the answers.

> Three clothespins plus two clothespins.
> **3 + 2 = 5**

If your child is quick to know the answers to these math problems, an occasional review may be all he or she needs. But if some of the answers come more slowly, it's a good idea to spend a few minutes each day having your child work with math facts at home.

Checkup 1

Left (Test A)

Name _____ Date _____

A.	0 $+\ 5$	3 $+\ 0$	2 $+\ 2$	3 $+\ 2$	2 $+\ 1$
B.	1 $+\ 3$	3 $+\ 1$	0 $+\ 3$	3 $+\ 1$	0 $+\ 4$
C.	5 $+\ 0$	1 $+\ 2$	2 $+\ 3$	1 $+\ 2$	4 $+\ 1$
D.	0 $+\ 2$	2 $+\ 0$	1 $+\ 1$	2 $+\ 0$	1 $+\ 0$
E.	2 $+\ 2$	5 $+\ 0$	3 $+\ 1$	5 $+\ 0$	1 $+\ 4$

Test A: Adding to 5

©The Education Center, Inc. • *Target Math Success* • TEC60825 • Key p. 135

Right (Test B)

Name _____ Date _____

A.	0 $+\ 3$	2 $+\ 2$	1 $+\ 4$	0 $+\ 4$	4 $+\ 1$
B.	3 $+\ 0$	1 $+\ 2$	5 $+\ 0$	3 $+\ 1$	2 $+\ 3$
C.	3 $+\ 2$	1 $+\ 3$	4 $+\ 0$	2 $+\ 1$	0 $+\ 5$
D.	0 $+\ 1$	1 $+\ 1$	2 $+\ 0$	0 $+\ 1$	0 $+\ 2$
E.	5 $+\ 0$	4 $+\ 1$	2 $+\ 3$	2 $+\ 1$	3 $+\ 2$

Test B: Adding to 5

©The Education Center, Inc. • *Target Math Success* • TEC60825 • Key p. 135

It's Time to Take Aim!

On _____ our class will be having a checkup on math facts. To help your child prepare, please spend about 15 minutes practicing math problems that review **adding to 6.** Thanks for your help!

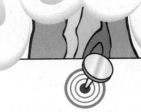

Target These!

1
0 + 1
1 + 0

2
0 + 2
1 + 1
2 + 0

3
0 + 3
1 + 2
2 + 1
3 + 0

4
0 + 4
1 + 3
2 + 2
3 + 1
4 + 0

5
0 + 5
1 + 4
2 + 3
3 + 2
4 + 1
5 + 0

6
0 + 6
1 + 5
2 + 4
3 + 3
4 + 2
5 + 1
6 + 0

On-Target Practice

Reviewing basic facts is quick and simple with this "hand-y" activity! Place six dry beans (or other small items) in your hand and show them to your child. Next, place your hands behind your back and move some of the beans to your other hand. Show your closed hands to your child. Open one hand and have him count the beans and write that number. Close that hand and then open your other hand and have him repeat the process. After he solves the problem, show him both open hands and have him count the beans to check his work. Continue playing by changing the number of beans in each hand. Now that's "sum-thing!"

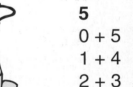

Great job!

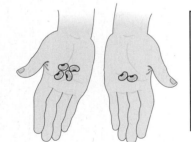

$4 + 2 = 6$

Wrap up by calling out the math problems at the right and having your child supply the answers.

If your child is quick to know the answers to these math problems, an occasional review may be all he or she needs. But if some of the answers come more slowly, it's a good idea to spend a few minutes each day having your child work with math facts at home.

Checkup 2

Checkup 2

Name _____   Date _____

Test B

A.	$\begin{array}{r}1\\+5\\\hline\end{array}$	$\begin{array}{r}1\\+2\\\hline\end{array}$	$\begin{array}{r}1\\+3\\\hline\end{array}$	$\begin{array}{r}4\\+2\\\hline\end{array}$ $\begin{array}{r}0\\+3\\\hline\end{array}$
B.	$\begin{array}{r}6\\+0\\\hline\end{array}$	$\begin{array}{r}2\\+4\\\hline\end{array}$	$\begin{array}{r}2\\+3\\\hline\end{array}$	$\begin{array}{r}4\\+0\\\hline\end{array}$ $\begin{array}{r}5\\+1\\\hline\end{array}$
C.	$\begin{array}{r}0\\+5\\\hline\end{array}$	$\begin{array}{r}1\\+1\\\hline\end{array}$	$\begin{array}{r}3\\+0\\\hline\end{array}$	$\begin{array}{r}0\\+2\\\hline\end{array}$ $\begin{array}{r}3\\+3\\\hline\end{array}$
D.	$\begin{array}{r}1\\+4\\\hline\end{array}$	$\begin{array}{r}2\\+2\\\hline\end{array}$	$\begin{array}{r}2\\+1\\\hline\end{array}$	$\begin{array}{r}1\\+0\\\hline\end{array}$ $\begin{array}{r}3\\+2\\\hline\end{array}$
E.	$\begin{array}{r}5\\+1\\\hline\end{array}$	$\begin{array}{r}4\\+2\\\hline\end{array}$	$\begin{array}{r}3\\+3\\\hline\end{array}$	$\begin{array}{r}2\\+0\\\hline\end{array}$ $\begin{array}{r}6\\+0\\\hline\end{array}$

Test B: Adding to 6

©The Education Center, Inc. • *Target Math Success* • TEC60825 • Key p. 135

Name _____   Date _____

Test A

A.	$\begin{array}{r}0\\+1\\\hline\end{array}$	$\begin{array}{r}2\\+4\\\hline\end{array}$	$\begin{array}{r}0\\+2\\\hline\end{array}$	$\begin{array}{r}5\\+1\\\hline\end{array}$
B.	$\begin{array}{r}1\\+1\\\hline\end{array}$	$\begin{array}{r}3\\+1\\\hline\end{array}$	$\begin{array}{r}0\\+3\\\hline\end{array}$	$\begin{array}{r}2\\+3\\\hline\end{array}$
C.	$\begin{array}{r}0\\+3\\\hline\end{array}$	$\begin{array}{r}1\\+5\\\hline\end{array}$	$\begin{array}{r}2\\+2\\\hline\end{array}$	$\begin{array}{r}1\\+0\\\hline\end{array}$
D.	$\begin{array}{r}3\\+3\\\hline\end{array}$	$\begin{array}{r}4\\+1\\\hline\end{array}$	$\begin{array}{r}3\\+2\\\hline\end{array}$	$\begin{array}{r}2\\+1\\\hline\end{array}$
E.	$\begin{array}{r}4\\+2\\\hline\end{array}$	$\begin{array}{r}1\\+3\\\hline\end{array}$	$\begin{array}{r}5\\+1\\\hline\end{array}$	$\begin{array}{r}2\\+3\\\hline\end{array}$

Test A: Adding to 6

©The Education Center, Inc. • *Target Math Success* • TEC60825 • Key p. 135

It's Time to Take Aim!

On _____ our class will be having a checkup on math facts. To help your child prepare, please spend about 15 minutes practicing math problems that review **adding to 7.** Thanks for your help!

Target These!

1	2	3
0 + 1	0 + 2	0 + 3
1 + 0	1 + 1	1 + 2
	2 + 0	2 + 1
		3 + 0

4	5	6
0 + 4	0 + 5	0 + 6
1 + 3	1 + 4	1 + 5
2 + 2	2 + 3	2 + 4
3 + 1	3 + 2	3 + 3
4 + 0	4 + 1	4 + 2
	5 + 0	5 + 1
		6 + 0

7

0 + 7
1 + 6
2 + 5
3 + 4
4 + 3
5 + 2
6 + 1
7 + 0

Four cotton balls plus three cotton balls.
4 + 3 = 7

On-Target Practice

Seven cotton balls and two shoelaces are just what you need to reinforce addition! Begin by asking your child to form a circle with each shoelace. Tell him to place four cotton balls in one circle and three cotton balls in the other circle. Then have him say the math fact the cotton balls represent *(4 + 3 = 7)*. After confirming his answer, have him remove the cotton balls. Repeat this activity using other number combinations that have sums up to seven.

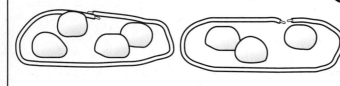

Wrap up by calling out the math problems at the right and having your child supply the answers.

If your child is quick to know the answers to these math problems, an occasional review may be all he or she needs. But if some of the answers come more slowly, it's a good idea to spend a few minutes each day having your child work with math facts at home.

Checkup 3

Name _____   Date _____

A.	6 + 1	3 + 2	0 + 5	2 + 5
B.	5 + 1	4 + 3	2 + 2	3 + 1
C.	1 + 6	2 + 1	6 + 0	4 + 1
D.	3 + 4	2 + 4	2 + 3	1 + 5
E.	2 + 2	1 + 5	5 + 2	0 + 7

Test A: Adding to 7

Checkup 3

Name _____   Date _____

A.	5 + 2	0 + 6	1 + 2	2 + 0	3 + 4
B.	5 − 0	2 + 5	3 + 3	1 + 6	4 + 0
C.	7 + 0	4 + 3	5 + 1	1 + 4	6 + 1
D.	4 + 2	0 + 4	1 + 3	3 + 2	0 + 7
E.	5 + 2	6 + 1	3 + 4	5 + 0	1 + 4

Test B: Adding to 7

It's Time to Take Aim!

On _____ our class will be having a checkup on math facts. To help your child prepare, please spend about 15 minutes practicing math problems that review **adding to 8.** Thanks for your help!

On-Target Practice

Here's a fun way to shake up math practice. Place eight red blocks and eight yellow blocks (or two similar sets of objects) in a bag. Ask your child to take eight blocks from the bag without looking. Then have him sort them and say a math fact that the blocks can represent. After confirming his answer, have him return the blocks to the bag and give the bag a good shake. Repeat this activity, having your child remove eight blocks several times, then seven, six, and five blocks repeatedly. Have him identify the math fact each set of blocks can represent.

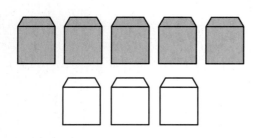

Wrap up by calling out the math problems at the right and having your child supply the answers.

Five red blocks plus three yellow blocks.
5 + 3 = 8

Target These!

1	2	3
0 + 1	0 + 2	0 + 3
1 + 0	1 + 1	1 + 2
	2 + 0	2 + 1
		3 + 0

4	5	6
0 + 4	0 + 5	0 + 6
1 + 3	1 + 4	1 + 5
2 + 2	2 + 3	2 + 4
3 + 1	3 + 2	3 + 3
4 + 0	4 + 1	4 + 2
	5 + 0	5 + 1
		6 + 0

7	8
0 + 7	0 + 8
1 + 6	1 + 7
2 + 5	2 + 6
3 + 4	3 + 5
4 + 3	4 + 4
5 + 2	5 + 3
6 + 1	6 + 2
7 + 0	7 + 1
	8 + 0

If your child is quick to know the answers to these math problems, an occasional review may be all he or she needs. But if some of the answers come more slowly, it's a good idea to spend a few minutes each day having your child work with math facts at home.

Checkup 4

Checkup 4

Name _____ Date _____

A.	2 +1	2 +5	1 +7	6 +2	3 +5
B.	2 +2	1 +4	4 +4	3 +3	0 +1
C.	2 +4	2 +6	1 +3	3 +4	1 +1
D.	2 +3	1 +5	5 +3	0 +3	1 +6
E.	4 +4	5 +0	3 +5	2 +6	3 +4

©The Education Center, Inc. • *Target Math Success* • TEC60825 • Key p. 136

Test A: Adding to 8

Checkup 4

Name _____ Date _____

A.	2 +2	2 +3	1 +5	5 +3	0 +3
B.	2 +1	1 +0	2 +5	1 +4	3 +5
C.	6 +2	1 +7	1 +3	4 +4	1 +6
D.	2 +4	3 +4	2 +6	1 +1	3 +3
E.	3 +1	4 +3	8 +0	1 +6	4 +4

©The Education Center, Inc. • *Target Math Success* • TEC60825 • Key p. 136

Test B: Adding to 8

It's Time to Take Aim!

On _____ our class will be having a checkup on math facts. To help your child prepare, please spend about 15 minutes practicing math problems that review **adding to 9.** Thanks for your help!

On-Target Practice

All you need for this counting-rope activity is one-half of a 32-inch shoelace and nine cereal pieces with holes in the middle. Knot the cut end of the shoelace; then thread the cereal onto it. Next, tie a knot at the opposite end of the shoelace, leaving plenty of room for the cereal to slide back and forth. Ask your child to slide six cereal pieces to one end of the shoelace. Then have him slide three more. Ask him to say the math fact the cereal pieces represent *(6 + 3 = 9)*. After confirming his answer, have him slide the cereal pieces back to the other end of the shoelace. Repeat this activity several more times, using the sums eight, seven, and six. Great job!

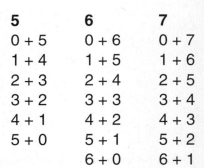

Wrap up by calling out the math problems at the right and having your child supply the answers.

> Seven cereal pieces plus one cereal piece.
> **7 + 1 = 8**

Target These!

2	3	4
0 + 2	0 + 3	0 + 4
1 + 1	1 + 2	1 + 3
2 + 0	2 + 1	2 + 2
	3 + 0	3 + 1
		4 + 0

5	6	7
0 + 5	0 + 6	0 + 7
1 + 4	1 + 5	1 + 6
2 + 3	2 + 4	2 + 5
3 + 2	3 + 3	3 + 4
4 + 1	4 + 2	4 + 3
5 + 0	5 + 1	5 + 2
	6 + 0	6 + 1
		7 + 0

8	9
0 + 8	0 + 9
1 + 7	1 + 8
2 + 6	2 + 7
3 + 5	3 + 6
4 + 4	4 + 5
5 + 3	5 + 4
6 + 2	6 + 3
7 + 1	7 + 2
8 + 0	8 + 1
	9 + 0

If your child is quick to know the answers to these math problems, an occasional review may be all he or she needs. But if some of the answers come more slowly, it's a good idea to spend a few minutes each day having your child work with math facts at home.

Checkup 5

Name Date

A.	1 +8	2 +6	3 +4	6 +1	5 +4
B.	9 +0	4 +5	1 +5	8 +1	3 +5
C.	6 +3	4 +4	7 +1	2 +7	0 +9
D.	5 +1	3 +6	7 +2	3 +3	5 +2
E.	1 +7	5 +3	8 +0	6 +2	4 +3

Checkup 5

Name Date

A.	5 +4	1 +7	2 +4	0 +6	4 +4
B.	8 +0	1 +8	4 +5	0 +7	5 +3
C.	3 +6	0 +9	6 +2	2 +5	2 +7
D.	7 +2	1 +6	8 +1	4 +2	6 +3
E.	9 +0	2 +6	0 +8	3 +5	3 +3

It's Time to Take Aim!

On _____ our class will be having a checkup on math facts. To help your child prepare, please spend about 15 minutes practicing math problems that review **adding to 10.** Thanks for your help!

Target These!

3	4	5
0 + 3	0 + 4	0 + 5
1 + 2	1 + 3	1 + 4
2 + 1	2 + 2	2 + 3
3 + 0	3 + 1	3 + 2
	4 + 0	4 + 1
		5 + 0

6	7	8
0 + 6	0 + 7	0 + 8
1 + 5	1 + 6	1 + 7
2 + 4	2 + 5	2 + 6
3 + 3	3 + 4	3 + 5
4 + 2	4 + 3	4 + 4
5 + 1	5 + 2	5 + 3
6 + 0	6 + 1	6 + 2
	7 + 0	7 + 1
		8 + 0

9	10
0 + 9	0 + 10
1 + 8	1 + 9
2 + 7	2 + 8
3 + 6	3 + 7
4 + 5	4 + 6
5 + 4	5 + 5
6 + 3	6 + 4
7 + 2	7 + 3
8 + 1	8 + 2
9 + 0	9 + 1
	10 + 0

On-Target Practice

Use a deck of cards to help your child review adding to 10 the fun way! Create a set of game cards by gathering the aces, twos, threes, fours, and fives from a deck of cards. Stack this partial card deck face down. Have your child flip over the top two cards, one at a time. Then ask him to say the math sentence the two cards represent (aces represent one). For example, if the cards are a four and a two, he would say, "4 + 2 = 6." Have him check his answer by counting the total number of symbols on both cards. Encourage your child to repeat this activity by turning over additional cards.

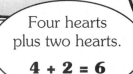

Four hearts plus two hearts.

$4 + 2 = 6$

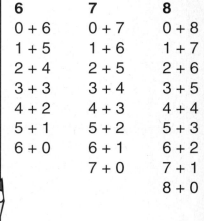

Wrap up by calling out the math problems at the right and having your child supply the answers.

If your child is quick to know the answers to these math problems, an occasional review may be all he or she needs. But if some of the answers come more slowly, it's a good idea to spend a few minutes each day having your child work with math facts at home.

Checkup 6

Name _____

A.
```
  2       5       1       3       4
+ 7     + 5     + 6     + 7     + 2
```

B.
```
  9       2       7       0       1
+ 1     + 5     + 3     +10     + 8
```

C.
```
  3       0       4       3       7
+ 4     + 9     + 6     + 6     + 1
```

D.
```
  6       0       4       0       8
+ 4     + 8     + 5     + 7     + 2
```

E.
```
  5       1       6       2       4
+ 3     + 9     + 2     + 8     + 4
```

Test A: Adding to 10

©The Education Center, Inc. • *Target Math Success* • TEC60825 • Key p. 136

Checkup 6

Name _____

Date _____

A.
```
  1       0       3       2       8
+ 7     +10     + 5     + 8     + 0
```

B.
```
  6       1       2       8       4
+ 3     + 9     + 4     + 1     + 4
```

C.
```
 10       4       9       9       6
+ 0     + 3     + 0     + 1     + 4
```

D.
```
  2       7       7       6       8
+ 6     + 2     + 3     + 1     + 2
```

E.
```
  5       5       4       5       3
+ 2     + 5     + 6     + 4     + 7
```

Test B: Adding to 10

©The Education Center, Inc. • *Target Math Success* • TEC60825 • Key p. 136

It's Time to Take Aim!

On _____ our class will be having a checkup on math facts. To help your child prepare, please spend about 15 minutes practicing math problems that review **adding to 11.** Thanks for your help!

On-Target Practice

Try this hands-on activity for a great math experience! Put two similar sets of 11 objects, such as 11 green M&M's candies and 11 brown M&M's candies, or two colors of cereal, together in a cup. Place your hand over the cup's opening and give it a gentle shake. Remove your hand and ask your child to randomly select 11 objects from the cup. Have him sort them and say the math fact the objects represent. Confirm his answer and have him return the objects to the cup. Then repeat this activity several more times. For more practice, have him repeat the activity in the same manner by removing ten, nine, and eight objects.

Wrap up by calling out the math problems at the right and having your child supply the answers.

Five green M&M's candies plus six brown M&M's candies.
5 + 6 = 11

Target These!

4	5	6
0 + 4	0 + 5	0 + 6
1 + 3	1 + 4	1 + 5
2 + 2	2 + 3	2 + 4
3 + 1	3 + 2	3 + 3
4 + 0	4 + 1	4 + 2
	5 + 0	5 + 1
		6 + 0

7	8	9
0 + 7	0 + 8	0 + 9
1 + 6	1 + 7	1 + 8
2 + 5	2 + 6	2 + 7
3 + 4	3 + 5	3 + 6
4 + 3	4 + 4	4 + 5
5 + 2	5 + 3	5 + 4
6 + 1	6 + 2	6 + 3
7 + 0	7 + 1	7 + 2
	8 + 0	8 + 1
		9 + 0

10	11
0 + 10	2 + 9
1 + 9	3 + 8
2 + 8	4 + 7
3 + 7	5 + 6
4 + 6	6 + 5
5 + 5	7 + 4
6 + 4	8 + 3
7 + 3	9 + 2
8 + 2	
9 + 1	
10 + 0	

If your child is quick to know the answers to these math problems, an occasional review may be all he or she needs. But if some of the answers come more slowly, it's a good idea to spend a few minutes each day having your child work with math facts at home.

Checkup 7

Name _____ Date _____

A. 4+5   3+8   8+3   7+2   2+8
B. 1+8   6+5   4+6   9+2   10+0
C. 4+7   7+3   2+9   9+1   3+8
D. 2+6   3+5   7+4   2+7   5+6
E. 5+3   0+10 8+1   0+9   3+6

Test A: Adding to 11

©The Education Center, Inc. • *Target Math Success* • TEC60825 • Key p. 136

Checkup 7

Name _____ Date _____

A. 7+1   3+8   3+7   0+9   4+7
B. 1+9   7+4   8+2   6+3   9+2
C. 5+6   6+4   8+3   1+9   5+4
D. 9+0   6+5   8+0   2+9   5+5
E. 3+6   8+1   0+10 5+3   6+2

Test B: Adding to 11

©The Education Center, Inc. • *Target Math Success* • TEC60825 • Key p. 136

It's Time to Take Aim!

On _____ our class will be having a checkup on math facts. To help your child prepare, please spend about 15 minutes practicing math problems that review **adding to 12.** Thanks for your help!

On-Target Practice

Dig out a set of double-six dominoes for a fun-filled, hands-on review of basic facts! Begin by placing the dominoes face down. Ask your child to choose a domino, turn it over, and say the number sentence the two sets of dots represent. Then have him check his answer by counting all the dots. Repeat this activity with the remaining dominoes. For additional practice, have your child sort the dominoes into number families, or combinations of dots that equal the same number. Is it fun to add up dots? Yes, lots!

Wrap up by calling out the math problems at the right and having your child supply the answers.

Five dots plus four dots.

$5 + 4 = 9$

Target These!

5	6	7
0 + 5	0 + 6	0 + 7
1 + 4	1 + 5	1 + 6
2 + 3	2 + 4	2 + 5
3 + 2	3 + 3	3 + 4
4 + 1	4 + 2	4 + 3
5 + 0	5 + 1	5 + 2
	6 + 0	6 + 1
		7 + 0

8	9	10
0 + 8	0 + 9	0 + 10
1 + 7	1 + 8	1 + 9
2 + 6	2 + 7	2 + 8
3 + 5	3 + 6	3 + 7
4 + 4	4 + 5	4 + 6
5 + 3	5 + 4	5 + 5
6 + 2	6 + 3	6 + 4
7 + 1	7 + 2	7 + 3
8 + 0	8 + 1	8 + 2
	9 + 0	9 + 1
		10 + 0

11	12
2 + 9	3 + 9
3 + 8	4 + 8
4 + 7	5 + 7
5 + 6	6 + 6
6 + 5	7 + 5
7 + 4	8 + 4
8 + 3	9 + 3
9 + 2	

If your child is quick to know the answers to these math problems, an occasional review may be all he or she needs. But if some of the answers come more slowly, it's a good idea to spend a few minutes each day having your child work with math facts at home.

Checkup 8

Name ____________________ Date __________

A.	3 + 7	5 + 7	2 + 9	4 + 6	7 + 5
B.	5 + 6	2 + 7	8 + 4	3 + 6	0 + 10
C.	3 + 5	1 + 9	4 + 8	5 + 2	2 + 6
D.	6 + 6	7 + 1	4 + 7	2 + 8	3 + 9
E.	3 + 8	4 + 4	1 + 8	9 + 3	5 + 5

Test A: Adding to 12

Checkup 8

Name ____________________ Date __________

A.	5 + 5	8 + 4	6 + 5	7 + 4	4 + 5
B.	9 + 1	8 + 3	7 + 3	10 + 0	4 + 8
C.	3 + 9	6 + 4	9 + 2	5 + 7	7 + 4
D.	6 + 2	6 + 5	5 + 3	7 + 5	8 + 1
E.	4 + 4	7 + 2	6 + 6	8 + 2	9 + 3

Test B: Adding to 12

It's Time to Take Aim!

On _____ our class will be having a checkup on math facts. To help your child prepare, please spend about 15 minutes practicing math problems that review **adding to 14.** Thanks for your help!

Target These!

7	8	9
0 + 7	0 + 8	0 + 9
1 + 6	1 + 7	1 + 8
2 + 5	2 + 6	2 + 7
3 + 4	3 + 5	3 + 6
4 + 3	4 + 4	4 + 5
5 + 2	5 + 3	5 + 4
6 + 1	6 + 2	6 + 3
7 + 0	7 + 1	7 + 2
	8 + 0	8 + 1
		9 + 0

10	11	12
0 + 10	2 + 9	3 + 9
1 + 9	3 + 8	4 + 8
2 + 8	4 + 7	5 + 7
3 + 7	5 + 6	6 + 6
4 + 6	6 + 5	7 + 5
5 + 5	7 + 4	8 + 4
6 + 4	8 + 3	9 + 3
7 + 3	9 + 2	
8 + 2		
9 + 1		
10 + 0		

13	14
4 + 9	5 + 9
5 + 8	6 + 8
6 + 7	7 + 7
7 + 6	8 + 6
8 + 5	9 + 5
9 + 4	

On-Target Practice

Here's a simple way to review adding numbers. Place a plain T-shirt on a flat surface. Lay a length of string or yarn across the middle of the T-shirt to divide it into two sections. Place 14 buttons in a bowl and place the bowl nearby. Tell your youngster to arrange some of the buttons on the top half of the T-shirt and some on the bottom half. Next, have him say the math fact the buttons represent. After confirming his answer, have him remove the buttons and return them to the bowl. Repeat this activity using other number combinations that review adding to 14.

Nine buttons plus five buttons.
9 + 5 = 14

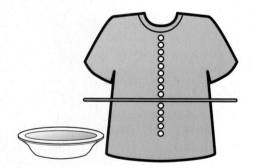

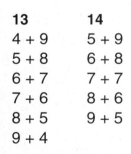

Wrap up by calling out the math problems at the right and having your child supply the answers.

If your child is quick to know the answers to these math problems, an occasional review may be all he or she needs. But if some of the answers come more slowly, it's a good idea to spend a few minutes each day having your child work with math facts at home.

Checkup 9

Name _____ Date _____

A.	6 +8	7 +5	6 +6	5 +9	4 +7
B.	5 +6	6 +7	3 +8	7 +7	5 +8
C.	8 +4	4 +9	8 +6	9 +3	7 +6
D.	9 +5	2 +9	8 +5	9 +4	5 +7
E.	1 +9	3 +7	4 +5	3 +9	4 +8

Test A: Adding to 14

©The Education Center, Inc. • Target Math Success • TEC60825 • Key p. 136

Checkup 9

Name _____ Date _____

A.	5 +8	4 +9	8 +2	3 +9	7 +7
B.	4 +8	6 +6	9 +5	7 +4	6 +5
C.	8 +5	6 +8	2 +9	6 +7	9 +4
D.	8 +6	5 +5	7 +6	2 +8	5 +9
E.	7 +3	6 +4	8 +3	5 +4	9 +3

Test B: Adding to 14

©The Education Center, Inc. • Target Math Success • TEC60825 • Key p. 136

It's Time to Take Aim!

On _____ our class will be having a checkup on math facts. To help your child prepare, please spend about 15 minutes practicing math problems that review **adding to 16.** Thanks for your help!

On-Target Practice

Shake up addition practice with this "eggs-tra" fun activity! Use a permanent marker to label the cups of an empty egg carton each with a number from 1 to 8. Place two beans (or similar item) in the carton and secure the lid. Give your child the prepared carton, a sheet of paper, and a pencil. Ask him to shake the carton, open the lid, and observe in which cups the beans settle. Then have him write the math fact that the two numbers represent. After confirming his answer, have him repeat this activity several times.

Wrap up by calling out the math problems at the right and having your child supply the answers.

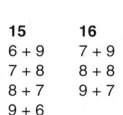

8 + 8 = 16

Target These!

9	10	11
0 + 9	0 + 10	2 + 9
1 + 8	1 + 9	3 + 8
2 + 7	2 + 8	4 + 7
3 + 6	3 + 7	5 + 6
4 + 5	4 + 6	6 + 5
5 + 4	5 + 5	7 + 4
6 + 3	6 + 4	8 + 3
7 + 2	7 + 3	9 + 2
8 + 1	8 + 2	
9 + 0	9 + 1	
	10 + 0	

12	13	14
3 + 9	4 + 9	5 + 9
4 + 8	5 + 8	6 + 8
5 + 7	6 + 7	7 + 7
6 + 6	7 + 6	8 + 6
7 + 5	8 + 5	9 + 5
8 + 4	9 + 4	
9 + 3		

15	16
6 + 9	7 + 9
7 + 8	8 + 8
8 + 7	9 + 7
9 + 6	

If your child is quick to know the answers to these math problems, an occasional review may be all he or she needs. But if some of the answers come more slowly, it's a good idea to spend a few minutes each day having your child work with math facts at home.

Checkup 10

Name _____   Date _____

A.
$\begin{array}{r} 7 \\ + 7 \\ \hline \end{array}$
$\begin{array}{r} 4 \\ + 9 \\ \hline \end{array}$
$\begin{array}{r} 7 \\ + 8 \\ \hline \end{array}$
$\begin{array}{r} 6 \\ + 6 \\ \hline \end{array}$
$\begin{array}{r} 5 \\ + 9 \\ \hline \end{array}$

B.
$\begin{array}{r} 6 \\ + 9 \\ \hline \end{array}$
$\begin{array}{r} 7 \\ + 6 \\ \hline \end{array}$
$\begin{array}{r} 3 \\ + 9 \\ \hline \end{array}$
$\begin{array}{r} 5 \\ + 7 \\ \hline \end{array}$
$\begin{array}{r} 7 \\ + 9 \\ \hline \end{array}$

C.
$\begin{array}{r} 8 \\ + 7 \\ \hline \end{array}$
$\begin{array}{r} 6 \\ + 7 \\ \hline \end{array}$
$\begin{array}{r} 6 \\ + 8 \\ \hline \end{array}$
$\begin{array}{r} 9 \\ + 5 \\ \hline \end{array}$
$\begin{array}{r} 8 \\ + 5 \\ \hline \end{array}$

D.
$\begin{array}{r} 8 \\ + 6 \\ \hline \end{array}$
$\begin{array}{r} 4 \\ + 8 \\ \hline \end{array}$
$\begin{array}{r} 8 \\ + 8 \\ \hline \end{array}$
$\begin{array}{r} 9 \\ + 2 \\ \hline \end{array}$
$\begin{array}{r} 5 \\ + 8 \\ \hline \end{array}$

E.
$\begin{array}{r} 9 \\ + 6 \\ \hline \end{array}$
$\begin{array}{r} 9 \\ + 4 \\ \hline \end{array}$
$\begin{array}{r} 8 \\ + 3 \\ \hline \end{array}$
$\begin{array}{r} 7 \\ + 4 \\ \hline \end{array}$
$\begin{array}{r} 9 \\ + 7 \\ \hline \end{array}$

Test A: Adding to 16

©The Education Center, Inc. • *Target Math Success* • TEC60825 • Key p. 136

Checkup 10

Name _____   Date _____

A.
$\begin{array}{r} 5 \\ + 8 \\ \hline \end{array}$
$\begin{array}{r} 8 \\ + 7 \\ \hline \end{array}$
$\begin{array}{r} 9 \\ + 5 \\ \hline \end{array}$
$\begin{array}{r} 7 \\ + 5 \\ \hline \end{array}$
$\begin{array}{r} 8 \\ + 8 \\ \hline \end{array}$

B.
$\begin{array}{r} 8 \\ + 6 \\ \hline \end{array}$
$\begin{array}{r} 4 \\ + 9 \\ \hline \end{array}$
$\begin{array}{r} 9 \\ + 6 \\ \hline \end{array}$
$\begin{array}{r} 7 \\ + 6 \\ \hline \end{array}$
$\begin{array}{r} 5 \\ + 9 \\ \hline \end{array}$

C.
$\begin{array}{r} 9 \\ + 7 \\ \hline \end{array}$
$\begin{array}{r} 2 \\ + 9 \\ \hline \end{array}$
$\begin{array}{r} 6 \\ + 5 \\ \hline \end{array}$
$\begin{array}{r} 7 \\ + 7 \\ \hline \end{array}$
$\begin{array}{r} 6 \\ + 9 \\ \hline \end{array}$

D.
$\begin{array}{r} 6 \\ + 8 \\ \hline \end{array}$
$\begin{array}{r} 8 \\ + 5 \\ \hline \end{array}$
$\begin{array}{r} 7 \\ + 9 \\ \hline \end{array}$
$\begin{array}{r} 6 \\ + 7 \\ \hline \end{array}$
$\begin{array}{r} 9 \\ + 3 \\ \hline \end{array}$

E.
$\begin{array}{r} 4 \\ + 8 \\ \hline \end{array}$
$\begin{array}{r} 9 \\ + 4 \\ \hline \end{array}$
$\begin{array}{r} 6 \\ + 6 \\ \hline \end{array}$
$\begin{array}{r} 7 \\ + 8 \\ \hline \end{array}$
$\begin{array}{r} 3 \\ + 8 \\ \hline \end{array}$

Test B: Adding to 16

©The Education Center, Inc. • *Target Math Success* • TEC60825 • Key p. 136

It's Time to Take Aim!

On _____ our class will be having a checkup on math facts. To help your child prepare, please spend about 15 minutes practicing math problems that reviewing **adding to 18.** Thanks for your help!

On-Target Practice

Using cotton swabs is a great way to practice addition! Place 18 cotton swabs next to two cups. Ask your child to count out nine cotton swabs and place them into one cup. Then have him count out nine more cotton swabs and place them into the other cup. Have him empty both cups and count the total number of cotton swabs. Ask him to say the math fact the cotton swabs represent *(9 + 9 = 18)*. After confirming his answer, repeat this activity several more times, using the sums 17, 16, and 15. Wow!

> Nine cotton swabs plus nine cotton swabs.
> **9 + 9 = 18**

Wrap up by calling out the math problems at the right and having your child supply the answers.

Target These!

11	12	13
2 + 9	3 + 9	4 + 9
3 + 8	4 + 8	5 + 8
4 + 7	5 + 7	6 + 7
5 + 6	6 + 6	7 + 6
6 + 5	7 + 5	8 + 5
7 + 4	8 + 4	9 + 4
8 + 3	9 + 3	
9 + 2		

14	15	16
5 + 9	6 + 9	7 + 9
6 + 8	7 + 8	8 + 8
7 + 7	8 + 7	9 + 7
8 + 6	9 + 6	
9 + 5		

17	18
8 + 9	9 + 9
9 + 8	

If your child is quick to know the answers to these math problems, an occasional review may be all he or she needs. But if some of the answers come more slowly, it's a good idea to spend a few minutes each day having your child work with math facts at home.

Checkup 11

Name _____

Date _____

A.
$$\begin{array}{r} 8 \\ +7 \\ \hline \end{array}$$
$$\begin{array}{r} 5 \\ +9 \\ \hline \end{array}$$
$$\begin{array}{r} 7 \\ +6 \\ \hline \end{array}$$
$$\begin{array}{r} 6 \\ +9 \\ \hline \end{array}$$
$$\begin{array}{r} 7 \\ +9 \\ \hline \end{array}$$

B.
$$\begin{array}{r} 6 \\ +8 \\ \hline \end{array}$$
$$\begin{array}{r} 9 \\ +9 \\ \hline \end{array}$$
$$\begin{array}{r} 5 \\ +8 \\ \hline \end{array}$$
$$\begin{array}{r} 9 \\ +5 \\ \hline \end{array}$$

C.
$$\begin{array}{r} 4 \\ +9 \\ \hline \end{array}$$
$$\begin{array}{r} 8 \\ +8 \\ \hline \end{array}$$
$$\begin{array}{r} 7 \\ +7 \\ \hline \end{array}$$
$$\begin{array}{r} 8 \\ +5 \\ \hline \end{array}$$
$$\begin{array}{r} 9 \\ +7 \\ \hline \end{array}$$

D.
$$\begin{array}{r} 9 \\ +6 \\ \hline \end{array}$$
$$\begin{array}{r} 6 \\ +7 \\ \hline \end{array}$$
$$\begin{array}{r} 9 \\ +8 \\ \hline \end{array}$$
$$\begin{array}{r} 8 \\ +6 \\ \hline \end{array}$$
$$\begin{array}{r} 9 \\ +4 \\ \hline \end{array}$$

E.
$$\begin{array}{r} 3 \\ +9 \\ \hline \end{array}$$
$$\begin{array}{r} 5 \\ +7 \\ \hline \end{array}$$
$$\begin{array}{r} 8 \\ +9 \\ \hline \end{array}$$
$$\begin{array}{r} 8 \\ +3 \\ \hline \end{array}$$
$$\begin{array}{r} 6 \\ +6 \\ \hline \end{array}$$

©The Education Center, Inc. • *Target Math Success* • TEC60825 • Key p. 136

Test A: Adding to 18

Checkup 11

Name _____

Date _____

A.
$$\begin{array}{r} 6 \\ +9 \\ \hline \end{array}$$
$$\begin{array}{r} 5 \\ +8 \\ \hline \end{array}$$
$$\begin{array}{r} 7 \\ +6 \\ \hline \end{array}$$
$$\begin{array}{r} 9 \\ +9 \\ \hline \end{array}$$
$$\begin{array}{r} 7 \\ +8 \\ \hline \end{array}$$

B.
$$\begin{array}{r} 5 \\ +9 \\ \hline \end{array}$$
$$\begin{array}{r} 8 \\ +8 \\ \hline \end{array}$$
$$\begin{array}{r} 4 \\ +9 \\ \hline \end{array}$$
$$\begin{array}{r} 8 \\ +6 \\ \hline \end{array}$$
$$\begin{array}{r} 8 \\ +9 \\ \hline \end{array}$$

C.
$$\begin{array}{r} 9 \\ +6 \\ \hline \end{array}$$
$$\begin{array}{r} 7 \\ +9 \\ \hline \end{array}$$
$$\begin{array}{r} 6 \\ +8 \\ \hline \end{array}$$
$$\begin{array}{r} 9 \\ +5 \\ \hline \end{array}$$
$$\begin{array}{r} 8 \\ +7 \\ \hline \end{array}$$

D.
$$\begin{array}{r} 6 \\ +7 \\ \hline \end{array}$$
$$\begin{array}{r} 9 \\ +8 \\ \hline \end{array}$$
$$\begin{array}{r} 7 \\ +7 \\ \hline \end{array}$$
$$\begin{array}{r} 8 \\ +5 \\ \hline \end{array}$$
$$\begin{array}{r} 9 \\ +7 \\ \hline \end{array}$$

E.
$$\begin{array}{r} 4 \\ +8 \\ \hline \end{array}$$
$$\begin{array}{r} 6 \\ +5 \\ \hline \end{array}$$
$$\begin{array}{r} 9 \\ +3 \\ \hline \end{array}$$
$$\begin{array}{r} 4 \\ +7 \\ \hline \end{array}$$
$$\begin{array}{r} 7 \\ +5 \\ \hline \end{array}$$

©The Education Center, Inc. • *Target Math Success* • TEC60825 • Key p. 136

Test B: Adding to 18

Aim high!

_____ knows the
basic addition facts

____ to ____!

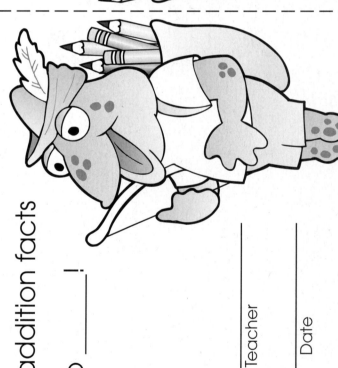

_____
Teacher

_____
Date

Right on target!

_____ knows the
basic addition facts

____ to ____!

_____
Teacher

_____
Date

Heigh-Ho! Off to Work We Go!

Name _____ Date _____

Add.

1 + 2 = 3   3 + 0 = 3

0 + 2 = 2   1 + 1 = 2

1 + 0 = 1   2 + 1 = 3

2 + 0 = 2   0 + 3 = 3

Colorful Facts

Name _____ Date _____

Add.
Color by the code.

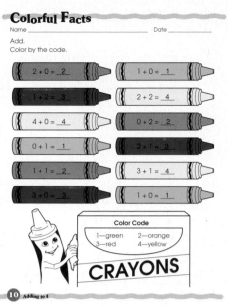

2 + 0 = 2   1 + 0 = 1

1 + 2 = 3   2 + 2 = 4

4 + 0 = 4   0 + 2 = 2

0 + 1 = 1   2 + 1 = 3

1 + 1 = 2   3 + 1 = 4

3 + 0 = 3   1 + 0 = 1

Color Code
1—green   2—orange
3—red   4—yellow

CRAYONS

Sun-Loving Lizards

Name _____ Date _____

Add.

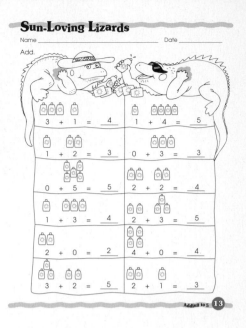

3 + 1 = 4   1 + 4 = 5

1 + 2 = 3   0 + 3 = 3

0 + 5 = 5   2 + 2 = 4

1 + 3 = 4   2 + 3 = 5

2 + 0 = 2   4 + 0 = 4

3 + 2 = 5   2 + 1 = 3

Lip-Licking Good!

Name _____ Date _____

Add.

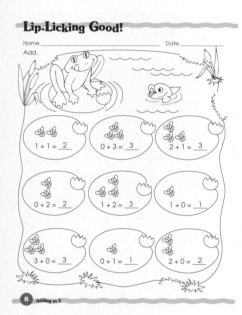

1 + 1 = 2   0 + 3 = 3   2 + 1 = 3

0 + 2 = 2   1 + 2 = 3   1 + 0 = 1

3 + 0 = 3   0 + 1 = 1   2 + 0 = 2

Honey, I'm Home!

Name _____ Date _____

Add.
Help Bee get the honey home.
If the answer is 3 or 4, color the cell yellow.

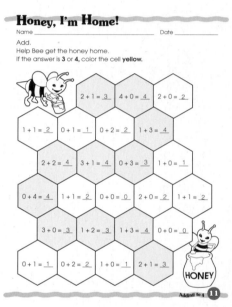

2 + 1 = 3   4 + 0 = 4   2 + 0 = 2

1 + 1 = 2   0 + 1 = 1   0 + 2 = 2   1 + 3 = 4

2 + 2 = 4   3 + 1 = 4   0 + 3 = 3   1 + 0 = 1

0 + 4 = 4   1 + 1 = 2   0 + 0 = 0   2 + 0 = 2   1 + 1 = 2

3 + 0 = 3   1 + 2 = 3   1 + 3 = 4   0 + 0 = 0

0 + 1 = 1   0 + 2 = 2   1 + 0 = 1   2 + 1 = 3

HONEY

Captain Quacker's Ship

Name _____ Date _____

Add.
Color by the code.

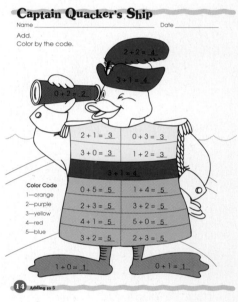

2 + 2 = 4

3 + 1 = 4

0 + 2 = 2

2 + 1 = 3   0 + 3 = 3

3 + 0 = 3   1 + 2 = 3

3 + 1 = 4

0 + 5 = 5   1 + 4 = 5

2 + 3 = 5   3 + 2 = 5

4 + 1 = 5   5 + 0 = 5

3 + 2 = 5   2 + 3 = 5

1 + 0 = 1   0 + 1 = 1

Color Code
1—orange
2—purple
3—yellow
4—red
5—blue

Field Goal Fun!

Name _____ Date _____

Add.

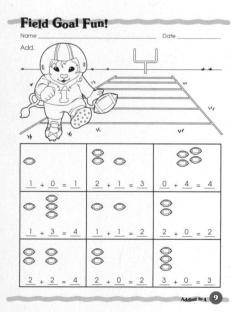

1 + 0 = 1   2 + 1 = 3   0 + 4 = 4

1 + 3 = 4   1 + 1 = 2   2 + 0 = 2

2 + 2 = 4   2 + 0 = 2   3 + 0 = 3

In the Moonlight

Name _____ Date _____

Add.
Color by the code.

Color Code
1 or 2—blue
3 or 4—yellow

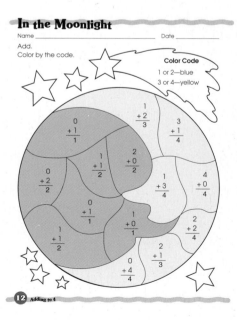

$\begin{array}{c} 0 \\ +1 \\ \hline 1 \end{array}$
$\begin{array}{c} 1 \\ +2 \\ \hline 3 \end{array}$
$\begin{array}{c} 3 \\ +1 \\ \hline 4 \end{array}$

$\begin{array}{c} 0 \\ +2 \\ \hline 2 \end{array}$
$\begin{array}{c} 2 \\ +0 \\ \hline 2 \end{array}$
$\begin{array}{c} 4 \\ +0 \\ \hline 4 \end{array}$

$\begin{array}{c} 0 \\ +1 \\ \hline 1 \end{array}$
$\begin{array}{c} 1 \\ +3 \\ \hline 4 \end{array}$

$\begin{array}{c} 1 \\ +2 \\ \hline \end{array}$
$\begin{array}{c} 1 \\ +0 \\ \hline 1 \end{array}$
$\begin{array}{c} 2 \\ +2 \\ \hline 4 \end{array}$

$\begin{array}{c} 2 \\ +1 \\ \hline 3 \end{array}$
$\begin{array}{c} 0 \\ +4 \\ \hline 4 \end{array}$

Squirrel's Super-size Snack

Name _____ Date _____

Add.
Help Squirrel get to the big acorn.
If the answer is 3 or 4, color the box green.

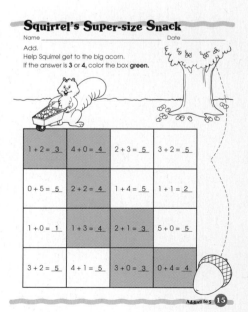

1 + 2 = 3   4 + 0 = 4   2 + 3 = 5   3 + 2 = 5

0 + 5 = 5   2 + 2 = 4   1 + 4 = 5   1 + 1 = 2

1 + 0 = 1   1 + 3 = 4   2 + 1 = 3   5 + 0 = 5

3 + 2 = 5   4 + 1 = 5   3 + 0 = 3   0 + 4 = 4

In Full Bloom

Name _____   Date _____

Add.
Color by the code.

Color Code
2—green   3—red
4—blue   5—yellow

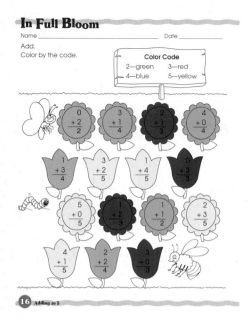

Gumball Surprises

Name _____   Date _____

Add.
Color by the code.

Color Code
1—purple   4—blue
2—red   5—green
3—orange   6—yellow

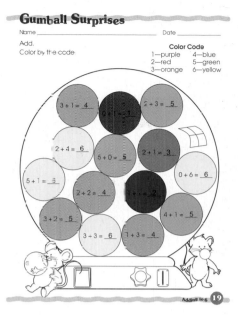

3 + 1 = 4
2 + 3 = 5
2 + 4 = 6
5 + 0 = 5
2 + 1 = 3
5 + 1 = 6
0 + 6 = 6
2 + 2 = 4
3 + 2 = 5
4 + 1 = 5
3 + 3 = 6
7 + 3 = 4

Making a Splash

Name _____   Date _____

Add.
Color by the code.

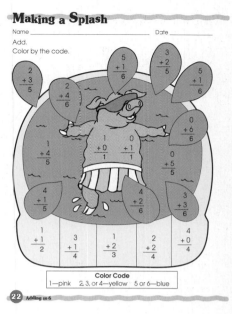

Color Code
1—pink   2, 3, or 4—yellow   5 or 6—blue

Munch Buddies

Name _____   Date _____

Add.
Color the matching number of peanuts.

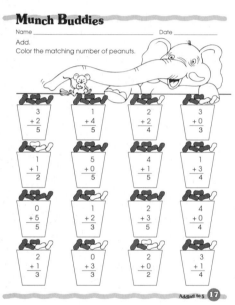

Where's My Bone?

Name _____   Date _____

Add.
Help Max find his bone.
If the answer is **5** or **6**, color the box **green**.

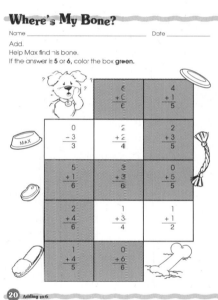

In the "Moo-d" for Ice Cream

Name _____   Date _____

Read.
Write the math sentence.

Cow eats 2 🍦s. She eats 2 more. How many 🍦s in all?	Cow has 2 🍦s. She makes 3 more. How many 🍦s in all?
2 + 2 = 4	2 + 3 = 5
Cow makes 5 🥤s. She makes 1 more. How many 🥤s in all?	Cow has 3 🍫s. She buys 3 more. How many 🍫s in all?
5 + 1 = 6	3 + 3 = 6
Cow has 2 🍦s. She eats 4 more. How many 🍦s in all?	Cow has 4 🍩s. She gets 1 more. How many 🍩s in all?
2 + 4 = 6	4 + 1 = 5

Going for a Swim

Name _____   Date _____

Add.

Remember: Adding two numbers in a different **order** does not change the sum.

1 + 0 = 1
0 + 1 = 1
2 + 0 = 2
0 + 2 = 2
5 + 0 = 5
0 + 5 = 5
0 + 4 = 4
4 + 0 = 4
3 + 1 = 4
1 + 3 = 4
0 + 3 = 3
3 + 0 = 3
1 + 2 = 3
2 + 1 = 3
2 + 3 = 5
3 + 2 = 5

Garden Helper

Name _____   Date _____

Add.
Color by the code.

Color Code
1 or 2—black   5—red
3 or 4—yellow   6—green

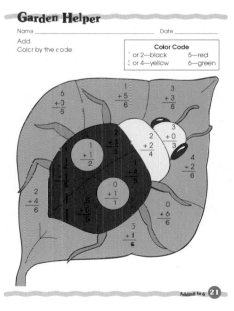

Party Under the Sea

Name _____   Date _____

Read.
Write the math sentence.

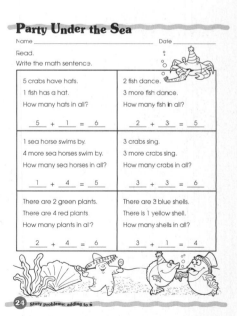

5 crabs have hats. 1 fish has a hat. How many hats in all?	2 fish dance. 3 more fish dance. How many fish in all?
5 + 1 = 6	2 + 3 = 5
1 sea horse swims by. 4 more sea horses swim by. How many sea horses in all?	3 crabs sing. 3 more crabs sing. How many crabs in all?
1 + 4 = 5	3 + 3 = 6
There are 2 green plants. There are 4 red plants. How many plants in all?	There are 3 blue shells. There is 1 yellow shell. How many shells in all?
2 + 4 = 6	3 + 1 = 4

Banana Fort Buddies

Name _____ Date _____

Add.
Color by the code.

Color Code
4 or 5—yellow
6 or 7—green

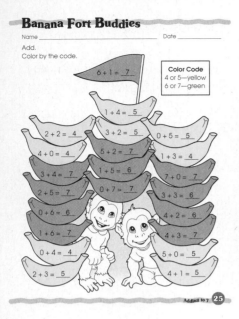

6 + 1 = _7_

1 + 4 = _5_

2 + 2 = _4_   3 + 2 = _5_   0 + 5 = _5_

4 + 0 = _4_   5 + 2 = _7_   1 + 3 = _4_

3 + 4 = _7_   1 + 5 = _6_   7 + 0 = _7_

2 + 5 = _7_   0 + 7 = _7_   3 + 3 = _6_

0 + 6 = _6_   4 + 2 = _6_

1 + 6 = _7_   4 + 3 = _7_

0 + 4 = _4_   5 + 0 = _5_

2 + 3 = _5_   4 + 1 = _5_

Barnyard Hide-and-Seek

Name _____ Date _____

Add.
Color by the code.

Color Code
1, 2, or 3—brown
4 or 5—yellow
6 or 7—red

Cookie Creatures

Name _____ Date _____

Read each big number.
Circle 4 ways to make that number.

5
1 + 3
(5 + 0)
(3 + 2)
2 + 2
(1 + 4)
(2 + 3)

6
(0 + 6)
(1 + 5)
4 + 1
(4 + 2)
1 + 1
3 + 3

7
(1 + 6)
0 + 5
(7 + 0)
1 + 2
(3 + 4)
(5 + 2)

8
2 + 5
(1 + 7)
(6 + 2)
4 + 0
(4 + 4)
3 + 5

Mouse's Midnight Munchies

Name _____ Date _____

Add.
Help hungry Mouse find the cheese.
If the answer is **6** or **7**, color the box **yellow**.

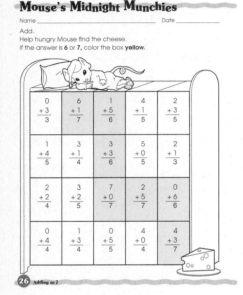

0 +3 = 3	6 +1 = 7	1 +5 = 6	4 +1 = 5	2 +3 = 5
1 +4 = 5	3 +1 = 4	3 +3 = 6	5 +0 = 5	2 +1 = 3
2 +2 = 4	3 +2 = 5	7 +0 = 7	2 +5 = 7	0 +6 = 6
0 +4 = 4	1 +3 = 4	0 +5 = 5	4 +0 = 4	4 +3 = 7

What a Smile!

Name _____ Date _____

Read.
Add.
Color by the code.

How many muscles does it take to smile?

Color Code
3 or 4—red
5, 6, or 7—green

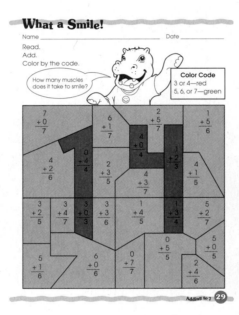

Fun in the Sun

Name _____ Date _____

Add.
Color by the code.

Color Code
4—brown
5—green
6—yellow
7—blue
8—red

Honey, Sweet Honey

Name _____ Date _____

Add.
Color by the code.

Color Code
4—purple   6—blue
5—red   7—yellow

Repeat After Me

Name _____ Date _____

Add.

Remember:
Adding two numbers in a different **order** does not change the sum.

| 5 + 2 = _7_ | 0 + 5 = _5_ | 2 + 4 = _6_ | 0 + 6 = _6_ |
| 2 + 5 = _7_ | 5 + 0 = _5_ | 4 + 2 = _6_ | 6 + 0 = _6_ |

| 0 + 3 = _3_ | 7 + 0 = _7_ | 1 + 5 = _6_ | 3 + 1 = _4_ |
| 3 + 0 = _3_ | 0 + 7 = _7_ | 5 + 1 = _6_ | 1 + 3 = _4_ |

| 4 + 1 = _5_ | 0 + 2 = _2_ | 4 + 3 = _7_ | 1 + 2 = _3_ |
| 1 + 4 = _5_ | 2 + 0 = _2_ | 3 + 4 = _7_ | 2 + 1 = _3_ |

| 0 + 1 = _1_ | 2 + 3 = _5_ | 4 + 0 = _4_ | 1 + 6 = _7_ |
| 1 + 0 = _1_ | 3 + 2 = _5_ | 0 + 4 = _4_ | 6 + 1 = _7_ |

What's Poppin'?

Name _____ Date _____

Add.
If the answer is **8**, color it **yellow**.

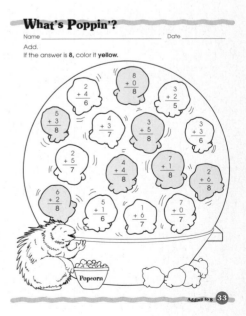

Picnic Path

Name _____ Date _____

Add.
Help the ant find the food.
If the answer is 7 or 8, color the box **red**.

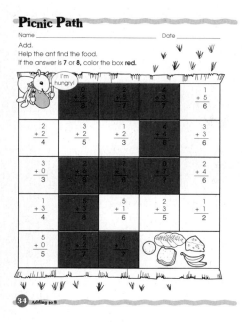

I'm hungry!

$\begin{array}{r}0\\+8\\\hline 8\end{array}$	$\begin{array}{r}2\\+5\\\hline 7\end{array}$	$\begin{array}{r}4\\+3\\\hline 7\end{array}$	$\begin{array}{r}1\\+5\\\hline 6\end{array}$
$\begin{array}{r}2\\+2\\\hline 4\end{array}$	$\begin{array}{r}3\\+2\\\hline 5\end{array}$	$\begin{array}{r}1\\+2\\\hline 3\end{array}$	$\begin{array}{r}4\\+4\\\hline 8\end{array}$	$\begin{array}{r}3\\+3\\\hline 6\end{array}$
$\begin{array}{r}3\\+0\\\hline 3\end{array}$	$\begin{array}{r}+6\\\hline \end{array}$	$\begin{array}{r}+1\\\hline \end{array}$	$\begin{array}{r}0\\+7\\\hline 7\end{array}$	$\begin{array}{r}2\\+4\\\hline 6\end{array}$
$\begin{array}{r}1\\+3\\\hline 4\end{array}$		$\begin{array}{r}5\\+1\\\hline 6\end{array}$	$\begin{array}{r}2\\+3\\\hline 5\end{array}$	$\begin{array}{r}1\\+1\\\hline 2\end{array}$
$\begin{array}{r}5\\+0\\\hline 5\end{array}$				

34 Adding to 8

Up, Up, and Away!

Name _____ Date _____

Add.
Color by the code

Color Code
9—red   8—yellow
7—purple   6—green
5—orange

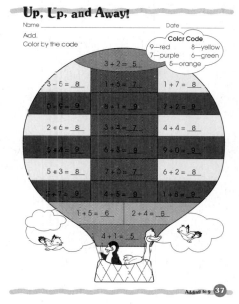

$3 + 2 = 5$

$3 - 5 = 8$ $1 + 5 = 7$ $1 + 7 = 8$

$0 - 5 = 9$ $8 + 1 = 9$ $7 + 2 = 9$

$2 + 6 = 8$ $3 + 4 = 7$ $4 + 4 = 8$

$5 + 4 = 9$ $6 + 3 = 9$ $9 + 0 = 9$

$5 + 3 = 8$ $7 + 0 = 7$ $6 + 2 = 8$

$+5 = 9$ $4 + 5 = 9$ $1 + 8 = 9$

$1 + 5 = 6$ $2 + 4 = 6$

$4 + 1 = 5$

Adding to 9 37

Horse on the Loose!

Name _____ Date _____

Add.
Help the cowboy find his horse.
If the answer is 8 or **9**, color the horseshoe **purple**.

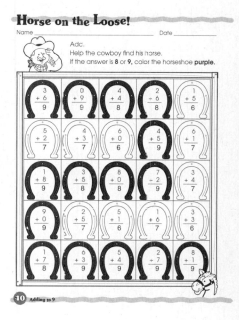

$\begin{array}{r}3\\+6\\\hline 9\end{array}$	$\begin{array}{r}0\\+9\\\hline 9\end{array}$	$\begin{array}{r}4\\+4\\\hline 8\end{array}$	$\begin{array}{r}2\\+6\\\hline 8\end{array}$	$\begin{array}{r}1\\+5\\\hline 6\end{array}$
$\begin{array}{r}5\\+2\\\hline 7\end{array}$	$\begin{array}{r}4\\+3\\\hline 7\end{array}$	$\begin{array}{r}6\\+0\\\hline 6\end{array}$	$\begin{array}{r}4\\+5\\\hline 9\end{array}$	$\begin{array}{r}6\\+1\\\hline 7\end{array}$
$\begin{array}{r}1\\+8\\\hline 9\end{array}$	$\begin{array}{r}3\\+5\\\hline 8\end{array}$	$\begin{array}{r}8\\+0\\\hline 8\end{array}$	$\begin{array}{r}7\\-2\\\hline \end{array}$	$\begin{array}{r}3\\+4\\\hline 7\end{array}$
$\begin{array}{r}9\\+0\\\hline 9\end{array}$	$\begin{array}{r}2\\+5\\\hline 7\end{array}$	$\begin{array}{r}3\\+6\\\hline 9\end{array}$	$\begin{array}{r}1\\+6\\\hline 7\end{array}$	$\begin{array}{r}5\\+3\\\hline 8\end{array}$
$\begin{array}{r}1\\+7\\\hline 8\end{array}$	$\begin{array}{r}6\\+3\\\hline 9\end{array}$	$\begin{array}{r}2\\+7\\\hline 9\end{array}$	$\begin{array}{r}2\\+7\\\hline 9\end{array}$	$\begin{array}{r}1\\+8\\\hline 9\end{array}$

10 Adding to 9

Camping Camels

Name _____ Date _____

Read.
Write the math sentence.

Carl Camel ate 3 hot dogs. He ate 2 more. How many hot dogs in all? $3 + 2 = 5$	Cathy Camel put 4 logs on the fire. She added 2 more. How many logs in all? $4 + 2 = 6$
Carl Camel sang 4 songs. He sang 4 more. How many songs in all? $4 + 4 = 8$	Cathy Camel caught 3 fish. She caught 4 more. How many fish in all? $3 + 4 = 7$
Carl Camel put up 5 tents. He put up 3 more. How many tents in all? $5 + 3 = 8$	The camels roasted 6 marshmallows. They roasted 1 more. How many marshmallows in all? $6 + 1 = 7$

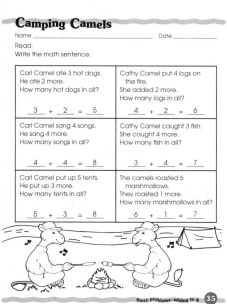

Story problems: adding to 8 35

Yummy for My Tummy

Name _____ Date _____

Add.
If the answer is **9**, color the carrot **orange**.

$\begin{array}{r}8\\+1\\\hline 9\end{array}$	$\begin{array}{r}2\\+6\\\hline 8\end{array}$	$\begin{array}{r}4\\+5\\\hline 9\end{array}$	$\begin{array}{r}6\\+1\\\hline 7\end{array}$	$\begin{array}{r}3\\+2\\\hline 5\end{array}$
$\begin{array}{r}5\\+2\\\hline 7\end{array}$	$\begin{array}{r}3\\+4\\\hline 7\end{array}$	$\begin{array}{r}6\\\\\hline 6\end{array}$	$\begin{array}{r}4\\+5\\\hline 9\end{array}$	$\begin{array}{r}0\\+9\\\hline 9\end{array}$
$\begin{array}{r}3\\+6\\\hline 9\end{array}$	$\begin{array}{r}5\\+0\\\hline \end{array}$	$\begin{array}{r}6\\+2\\\hline 8\end{array}$	$\begin{array}{r}3\\+4\\\hline 7\end{array}$	$\begin{array}{r}1\\+8\\\hline 9\end{array}$
$\begin{array}{r}5\\+4\\\hline 9\end{array}$	$\begin{array}{r}4\\+2\\\hline 6\end{array}$	$\begin{array}{r}3\\+5\\\hline 8\end{array}$	$\begin{array}{r}6\\+3\\\hline 9\end{array}$	$\begin{array}{r}6\\+0\\\hline 6\end{array}$

38 Adding to 9

Pigs at Work

Name _____ Date _____

Read each big number.
Circle 4 ways to make that number.

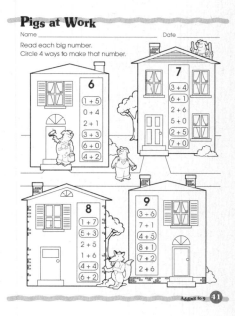

6
1 + 5
0 + 4
2 + 1
3 + 3
6 + 0
4 + 2

7
3 + 4
6 + 1
2 + 6
2 + 5
7 + 0

8
1 + 7
5 + 3
2 + 5
1 + 6
4 + 4
6 + 2

9
3 + 6
7 + 1
4 + 5
8 + 1
2 + 6

Adding to 9 41

Sam the Snoozing Snake

Name _____ Date _____

Read.
Write the math sentence.
Color by the code.

Ssss

Color Code
4—green   6—yellow
5—red   7—blue
8—orange

Sam sleeps for 4 hours. He sleeps for 4 more. How many hours in all?	There are 2 pillows. There are 2 more. How many pillows in all? $2 + 2 = 4$
Sam has 2 teddy bears. He gets 5 more. How many bears in all? $2 + 5 = 7$	Sam crawls 6 inches. He crawls 2 more. How many inches in all? $6 + 2 = 8$
Sam has 3 brothers. He has 3 sisters. How many in all? $3 + 3 = 6$	Sam sees 2 mice. He sees 3 more. How many mice in all? $2 + 3 = 5$
There is 1 red snake. There are 7 black snakes. How many snakes in all? $1 + 7 = 8$	Sam has 4 dreams. He has 3 more. How many dreams in all? $4 + 3 = 7$

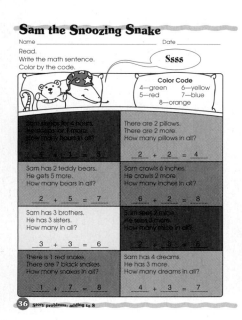

36 Story problems: adding to 8

Look Out Below!

Name _____ Date _____

Add.
Color by the code.

Color Code
9—pink
8—brown
7—green
6—purple
5—red
2, 3, or 4—yellow

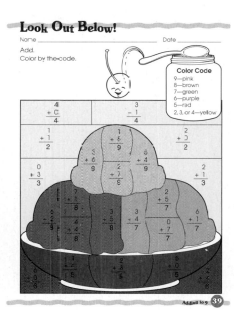

$\begin{array}{r}4\\+0\\\hline 4\end{array}$ $\begin{array}{r}3\\-1\\\hline 4\end{array}$

$\begin{array}{r}1\\+1\\\hline 2\end{array}$ $\begin{array}{r}1\\+8\\\hline 9\end{array}$ $\begin{array}{r}1\\+2\\\hline \end{array}$

$\begin{array}{r}0\\+3\\\hline 3\end{array}$ $\begin{array}{r}+6\\\hline \end{array}$ $\begin{array}{r}+4\\\hline \end{array}$ $\begin{array}{r}4\\+1\\\hline \end{array}$

$\begin{array}{r}3\\+5\\\hline 8\end{array}$ $\begin{array}{r}+5\\\hline 7\end{array}$ $\begin{array}{r}6\\+1\\\hline 7\end{array}$

Adding to 9 39

Lazy Day at the Pond

Name _____ Date _____

Add.

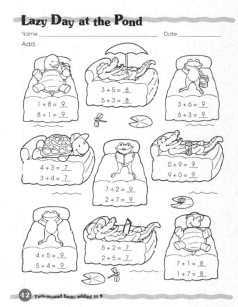

$1 + 8 = 9$
$8 + 1 = 9$

$3 + 5 = 8$
$5 + 3 = 8$

$3 + 6 = 9$
$6 + 3 = 9$

$4 + 3 = 7$
$3 + 4 = 7$

$0 + 9 = 9$
$9 + 0 = 9$

$7 + 2 = 9$
$2 + 7 = 9$

$4 + 5 = 9$
$5 + 4 = 9$

$5 + 2 = 7$
$2 + 5 = 7$

$7 + 1 = 8$
$1 + 7 = 8$

42 Turn-around facts: adding to 9

Smooth Sailing

Name _____ Date _____

Add.
Color by the code.

Color Code
5—blue   8—purple
6—red   9—orange
7—green   10—yellow

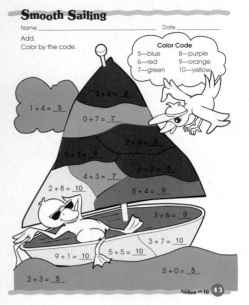

$1 + 4 = 5$

$3 + 3 = 6$

$0 + 7 = 7$

$2 + 4 = 6$

$5 + 3 = 8$

$6 + 2 = 8$

$4 + 3 = 7$

$2 + 8 = 10$

$5 + 4 = 9$

$3 + 6 = 9$

$3 + 7 = 10$

$9 + 1 = 10$

$5 + 5 = 10$

$5 + 0 = 5$

$2 + 3 = 5$

Adding to 10 **43**

Here a Chick! Where a Chick?

Name _____ Date _____

Add.
Help Mother Hen find her chicks.
If the answer is **10**, color the bag **brown**.

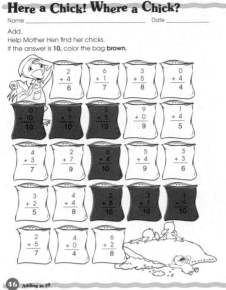

Row 1:
$\begin{array}{r}2\\+4\\\hline\end{array}$
$\begin{array}{r}6\\+1\\\hline 7\end{array}$
$\begin{array}{r}3\\+5\\\hline 8\end{array}$
$\begin{array}{r}0\\+4\\\hline 4\end{array}$

Row 2:
$\begin{array}{r}0\\+10\\\hline 10\end{array}$
$\begin{array}{r}9\\+1\\\hline 10\end{array}$
$\begin{array}{r}5\\+5\\\hline 10\end{array}$
$\begin{array}{r}9\\+0\\\hline 9\end{array}$
$\begin{array}{r}1\\+4\\\hline 5\end{array}$

Row 3:
$\begin{array}{r}4\\+3\\\hline 7\end{array}$
$\begin{array}{r}2\\+7\\\hline 9\end{array}$
$\begin{array}{r}6\\+4\\\hline 10\end{array}$
$\begin{array}{r}5\\+4\\\hline 9\end{array}$
$\begin{array}{r}3\\+3\\\hline 6\end{array}$

Row 4:
$\begin{array}{r}3\\+2\\\hline 5\end{array}$
$\begin{array}{r}4\\+4\\\hline 8\end{array}$
$\begin{array}{r}8\\+2\\\hline 10\end{array}$
$\begin{array}{r}3\\+7\\\hline 10\end{array}$
$\begin{array}{r}1\\+9\\\hline 10\end{array}$

Row 5:
$\begin{array}{r}2\\+5\\\hline 7\end{array}$
$\begin{array}{r}4\\+0\\\hline 4\end{array}$
$\begin{array}{r}6\\+2\\\hline 8\end{array}$

46 Adding to 10

Parrot's Treasure

Name _____ Date _____

Add.
Color by the code.

Color Code
8—red   10—blue
9—orange 11—purple

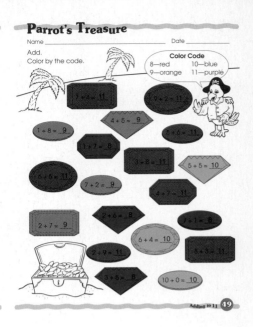

$7 + 4 = 11$

$9 + 2 = 11$

$4 + 5 = 9$

$1 + 8 = 9$

$5 + 6 = 11$

$1 + 7 = 8$

$3 + 8 = 11$

$5 + 5 = 10$

$6 + 5 = 11$

$7 + 2 = 9$

$4 + 7 = 11$

$2 + 7 = 9$

$2 + 6 = 8$

$7 + 1 = 8$

$6 + 4 = 10$

$2 + 11 = 11$

$8 + 3 = 11$

$3 + 5 = 8$

$10 + 0 = 10$

Adding to 11 **49**

A Touch of Color

Name _____ Date _____

Add.
Color by the code.

Color Code
7—blue
8—orange
9—yellow
10—red

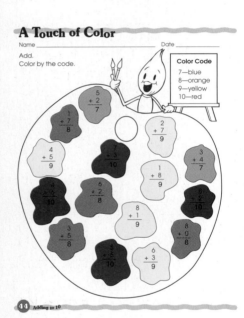

$\begin{array}{r}5\\+2\\\hline 7\end{array}$
$\begin{array}{r}1\\+7\\\hline 8\end{array}$
$\begin{array}{r}2\\+7\\\hline 9\end{array}$
$\begin{array}{r}4\\+5\\\hline 9\end{array}$
$\begin{array}{r}7\\+3\\\hline 10\end{array}$
$\begin{array}{r}3\\+4\\\hline 7\end{array}$
$\begin{array}{r}1\\+8\\\hline 9\end{array}$
$\begin{array}{r}4\\+6\\\hline 10\end{array}$
$\begin{array}{r}6\\+2\\\hline 8\end{array}$
$\begin{array}{r}2\\+10\\\hline 10\end{array}$
$\begin{array}{r}8\\+1\\\hline 9\end{array}$
$\begin{array}{r}3\\+5\\\hline 8\end{array}$
$\begin{array}{r}8\\+0\\\hline 8\end{array}$
$\begin{array}{r}5\\+5\\\hline 10\end{array}$
$\begin{array}{r}6\\+3\\\hline 9\end{array}$

44 Adding to 10

Hanging Out at the Castle

Name _____ Date _____

Read.
Write the math sentence.

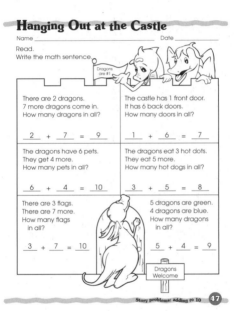

Dragons are #1

There are 2 dragons.
7 more dragons come in.
How many dragons in all?

$2 + 7 = 9$

The castle has 1 front door.
It has 6 back doors.
How many doors in all?

$1 + 6 = 7$

The dragons have 6 pets.
They get 4 more.
How many pets in all?

$6 + 4 = 10$

The dragons eat 3 hot dots.
They eat 5 more.
How many hot dogs in all?

$3 + 5 = 8$

There are 3 flags.
There are 7 more.
How many flags in all?

$3 + 7 = 10$

5 dragons are green.
4 dragons are blue.
How many dragons in all?

$5 + 4 = 9$

Dragons Welcome

Story problems: adding to 10 **47**

Hip-Hop Polar Pals

Name _____ Date _____

Add.
Match the letters to the numbered lines below to solve the riddle.

What did the polar bear say when he saw his penguin friend?

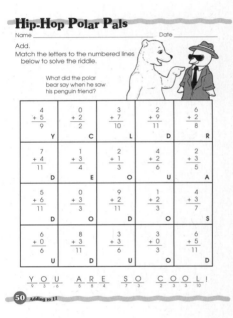

$\begin{array}{r}4\\+5\\\hline 9\end{array}$ Y	$\begin{array}{r}0\\+2\\\hline 2\end{array}$ C	$\begin{array}{r}3\\+7\\\hline 10\end{array}$ L	$\begin{array}{r}2\\+9\\\hline 11\end{array}$ D	$\begin{array}{r}6\\+2\\\hline 8\end{array}$ R
$\begin{array}{r}7\\+4\\\hline 11\end{array}$ D	$\begin{array}{r}1\\+3\\\hline 4\end{array}$ E	$\begin{array}{r}2\\+1\\\hline 3\end{array}$ O	$\begin{array}{r}4\\+2\\\hline 6\end{array}$ U	$\begin{array}{r}3\\+2\\\hline 5\end{array}$ A
$\begin{array}{r}5\\+6\\\hline 11\end{array}$ D	$\begin{array}{r}0\\+3\\\hline 3\end{array}$ O	$\begin{array}{r}9\\+2\\\hline 11\end{array}$ D	$\begin{array}{r}1\\+2\\\hline 3\end{array}$ O	$\begin{array}{r}4\\+3\\\hline 7\end{array}$ S
$\begin{array}{r}6\\+0\\\hline 6\end{array}$ U	$\begin{array}{r}8\\+3\\\hline 11\end{array}$ D	$\begin{array}{r}3\\+3\\\hline 6\end{array}$ U	$\begin{array}{r}3\\+0\\\hline 3\end{array}$ O	$\begin{array}{r}6\\+5\\\hline 11\end{array}$ D

$\underset{9\ 3\ 6}{Y\ O\ U}$ $\underset{5\ 8\ 4}{A\ R\ E}$ $\underset{7\ 3}{S\ O}$ $\underset{2\ 3\ 10}{C\ O\ O\ L}$!

50 Adding to 11

Them Bones

Name _____ Date _____

There are 206 bones in an adult body. But how many bones are in your body when you are born?

Add.
If the answer is **9** or **10**, color it **yellow**.

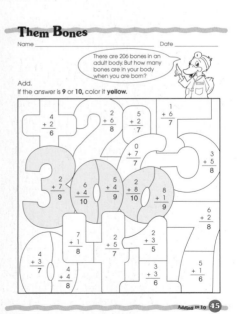

$\begin{array}{r}4\\+2\\\hline 6\end{array}$
$\begin{array}{r}1\\+6\\\hline 7\end{array}$
$\begin{array}{r}2\\+6\\\hline 8\end{array}$
$\begin{array}{r}5\\+2\\\hline 7\end{array}$
$\begin{array}{r}0\\+7\\\hline 7\end{array}$
$\begin{array}{r}3\\+5\\\hline 8\end{array}$
$\begin{array}{r}3\\+6\\\hline 9\end{array}$
$\begin{array}{r}2\\+7\\\hline 9\end{array}$
$\begin{array}{r}6\\+4\\\hline 10\end{array}$
$\begin{array}{r}5\\+4\\\hline 9\end{array}$
$\begin{array}{r}2\\+8\\\hline 10\end{array}$
$\begin{array}{r}4\\+1\\\hline 5\end{array}$
$\begin{array}{r}6\\+2\\\hline 8\end{array}$
$\begin{array}{r}7\\+1\\\hline 8\end{array}$
$\begin{array}{r}2\\+5\\\hline 7\end{array}$
$\begin{array}{r}2\\+3\\\hline 5\end{array}$
$\begin{array}{r}4\\+3\\\hline 7\end{array}$
$\begin{array}{r}4\\+4\\\hline 8\end{array}$
$\begin{array}{r}3\\+3\\\hline 6\end{array}$
$\begin{array}{r}5\\+1\\\hline 6\end{array}$

Adding to 10 **45**

Schoolhouse Sums

Name _____ Date _____

Read.
Write the math sentence.

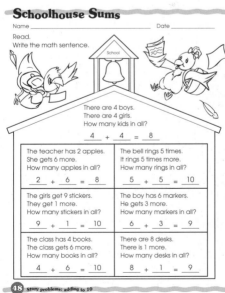

School

There are 4 boys.
There are 4 girls.
How many kids in all?

$4 + 4 = 8$

The teacher has 2 apples.
She gets 6 more.
How many apples in all?

$2 + 6 = 8$

The bell rings 5 times.
It rings 5 times more.
How many rings in all?

$5 + 5 = 10$

The girls get 9 stickers.
They get 1 more.
How many stickers in all?

$9 + 1 = 10$

The boy has 6 markers.
He gets 3 more.
How many markers in all?

$6 + 3 = 9$

The class has 4 books.
The class gets 6 more.
How many books in all?

$4 + 6 = 10$

There are 8 desks.
There is 1 more.
How many desks in all?

$8 + 1 = 9$

48 Story problems: adding to 10

Chow Time!

Name _____ Date _____

Add.
Color by the code.

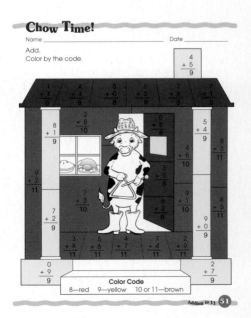

$\begin{array}{r}4\\+5\\\hline 9\end{array}$
$\begin{array}{r}1\\+7\\\hline 8\end{array}$
$\begin{array}{r}1\\+4\\\hline\end{array}$
$\begin{array}{r}9\\+1\\\hline\end{array}$
$\begin{array}{r}7\\+4\\\hline 11\end{array}$
$\begin{array}{r}8\\+1\\\hline 9\end{array}$
$\begin{array}{r}2\\+8\\\hline 10\end{array}$
$\begin{array}{r}5\\+4\\\hline 9\end{array}$
$\begin{array}{r}6\\+4\\\hline 10\end{array}$
$\begin{array}{r}3\\+8\\\hline 11\end{array}$
$\begin{array}{r}9\\+2\\\hline 11\end{array}$
$\begin{array}{r}5\\+3\\\hline 8\end{array}$
$\begin{array}{r}6\\+2\\\hline 8\end{array}$
$\begin{array}{r}7\\+2\\\hline 9\end{array}$
$\begin{array}{r}9\\+0\\\hline 9\end{array}$
$\begin{array}{r}6\\+5\\\hline 11\end{array}$
$\begin{array}{r}0\\+9\\\hline\end{array}$
$\begin{array}{r}2\\+7\\\hline\end{array}$

Color Code
8—red   9—yellow   10 or 11—brown

Adding to 11 **51**

Par for the Course!

Name _____ Date _____

Add.
Gopher needs to find the next golf tee.
If the answer is **10** or **11**, color the box
brown to make a tunnel.

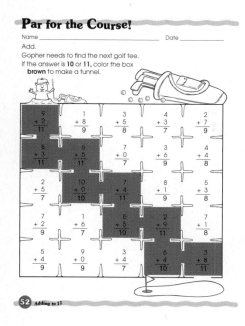

9 + 2 = 11	1 + 8 = 9	3 + 5 = 8	4 + 3 = 7	2 + 7 = 9
8 + 3 = 11	6 + 5 = 11	7 + 0 = 7	3 + 6 = 9	4 + 4 = 8
2 + 5 = 7	10 + 0 = 10	7 + 4 = 11	8 + 1 = 9	5 + 3 = 8
7 + 2 = 9	1 + 6 = 7	5 + 5 = 10	2 + 9 = 11	7 + 1 = 8
5 + 4 = 9	9 + 0 = 9	3 + 4 = 7	6 + 4 = 10	3 + 8 = 11

Monkey Island

Name _____ Date _____

Add.
Color by the code

Color Code
8—black   9—brown   10—blue   11—green   12—yellow

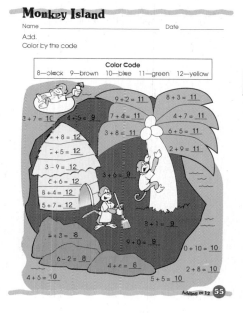

9 + 2 = 11   8 + 3 = 11
3 + 7 = 10   4 + 5 = 9   7 + 4 = 11   4 + 7 = 11
4 + 8 = 12   3 + 8 = 11   6 + 5 = 11
7 + 5 = 12   2 + 9 = 11
3 - 9 = 12
6 + 6 = 12   3 + 6 = 9
8 + 4 = 12
5 + 7 = 12
3 + 1 = 9
3 + 3 = 8
9 + 0 = 9
6 - 2 = 8   4 + 6 = 8   0 + 10 = 10
4 + 6 = 10   2 + 8 = 10
5 + 5 = 10

Riddle Roundup

Name _____ Date _____

Add.
Write the matching letters from the code.
Read the riddle answer.

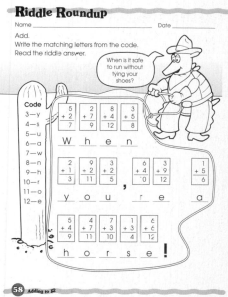

When is it safe
to run without
tying your shoes?

Code
3—y
4—s
5—u
6—a
7—w
8—n
9—n
10—r
11—o
12—e

W h e n

y o u ' r e   a

h o r s e !

Mouse on the Moon!

Name _____ Date _____

Add.
Cross out a matching answer.

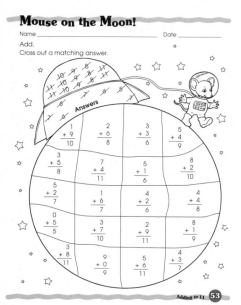

Answers

1 + 9 = 10	2 + 6 = 8	3 + 3 = 6	5 + 4 = 9
3 + 5 = 8	7 + 4 = 11	5 + 1 = 6	8 + 2 = 10
5 + 2 = 7	1 + 6 = 7	4 + 2 = 6	4 + 4 = 8
0 + 5 = 5	3 + 7 = 10	2 + 9 = 11	8 + 1 = 9
3 + 8 = 11	0 + 9 = 9	5 + 6 = 11	4 + 3 = 7

Hopping Off to School

Name _____ Date _____

Add.
Help Joey get to school.
If the answer is **11** or **12**, color it **green**.

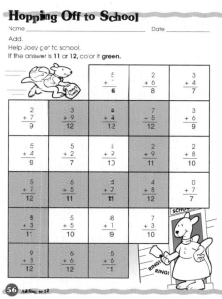

3...2...1... Blast Off

Name _____ Date _____

Write the math sentence.

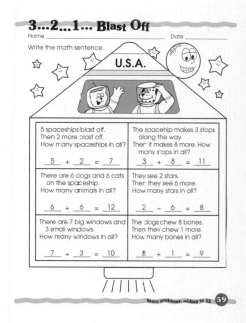

U.S.A.

5 spaceships blast off. Then 2 more blast off. How many spaceships in all? $5 + 2 = 7$	The spaceship makes 3 stops along the way. Then it makes 8 more. How many stops in all? $3 + 8 = 11$
There are 6 dogs and 6 cats on the spaceship. How many animals in all? $6 + 6 = 12$	They see 2 stars. Then they see 6 more. How many stars in all? $2 - 6 = 8$
There are 7 big windows and 3 small windows. How many windows in all? $7 + 3 = 10$	The dogs chew 8 bones. Then they chew 1 more. How many bones in all? $8 + 1 = 9$

Catnap

Name _____ Date _____

Add.

1 + 9 = 10   3 + 8 = 11   4 + 6 = 10
9 + 1 = 10   8 + 3 = 11   6 + 4 = 10

9 + 2 = 11   4 + 7 = 11   10 + 0 = 10
2 + 9 = 11   7 + 4 = 11   0 + 10 = 10

3 + 7 = 10   5 + 6 = 11   2 + 8 = 10
7 + 3 = 10   6 + 5 = 11   8 + 2 = 10

Dive Right In!

Name _____ Date _____

Add.
Cross off a matching answer.

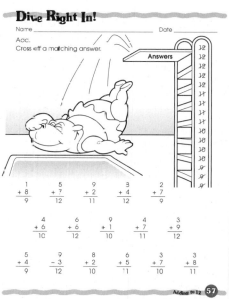

Answers

12 12 12 12 12 11 11 11 10 10 10 10

1 + 8 = 9	5 + 7 = 12	9 + 2 = 11	3 + 4 = 7	2 + 7 = 9
4 + 6 = 10	6 + 6 = 12	9 + 1 = 10	4 + 7 = 11	3 + 9 = 12
5 + 4 = 9	9 - 3 = 6	8 + 2 = 10	6 + 5 = 11	3 + 8 = 11

Race to the Finish Line

Name _____ Date _____

Write the math sentence.

Start   Finish

There are 5 races. There are 5 more. How many races in all? $5 + 5 = 10$	7 cars are in a race. 5 more cars race. How many cars in all? $7 + 5 = 12$
They change 6 tires. They change 4 more. How many tires in all? $6 + 4 = 10$	The cars make 4 laps. They make 8 more. How many laps in all? $4 + 8 = 12$
They wave 6 flags. Then they wave 5 more. How many flags in all? $6 + 5 = 11$	3 people are at the race. 9 more people come. How many people in all? $3 + 9 = 12$
4 people fix the car. 7 more people help. How many people in all? $4 + 7 = 11$	There are 6 red cars. There are 6 blue cars. How many cars in all? $6 + 6 = 12$

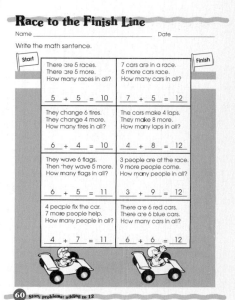

A Rain Forest Friend

Name _____ Date _____

Add.
Color by the code.

Color Code
7—brown 8—red 9—blue
10 or 11—green 12 or 13—black
14—white

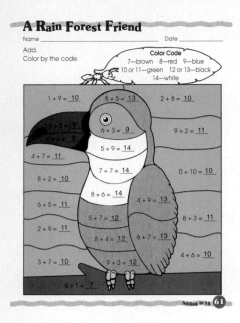

$1 + 9 = 10$
$8 + 5 = 13$
$2 + 8 = 10$
$6 + 3 = 9$
$9 + 2 = 11$
$5 + 9 = 14$
$7 + 7 = 14$
$0 + 10 = 10$
$8 + 2 = 10$
$4 + 7 = 11$
$8 + 6 = 14$
$4 + 9 = 13$
$6 + 5 = 11$
$8 + 3 = 11$
$5 + 7 = 12$
$2 + 9 = 11$
$8 + 4 = 12$
$6 + 7 = 13$
$4 + 6 = 10$
$3 + 7 = 10$
$9 + 3 = 12$
$6 + 1 = 7$

Send Me a Letter

Name _____ Date _____

Add.
Match the letters to the numbered lines
below to solve the riddle.

What do you call two pigs that
write each other letters?

4 $+9$ $\overline{13}$ **L**	8 $+6$ $\overline{14}$ **P**	5 $+4$ $\overline{9}$ **G**	2 $+8$ $\overline{10}$ **O**	7 $+7$ $\overline{14}$ **P**
7 $+3$ $\overline{10}$ **S**	9 $+5$ $\overline{14}$ **P**	3 $+9$ $\overline{12}$ **I**	9 $+0$ $\overline{9}$ **S**	4 $+7$ $\overline{11}$ **G**
2 $+9$ $\overline{11}$ **A**	5 $+3$ $\overline{8}$ **O**	10 $+0$ $\overline{10}$ **S**	4 $+4$ $\overline{8}$ **O**	6 $+3$ $\overline{9}$ **A**
6 $+6$ $\overline{12}$ **S**	6 $+4$ $\overline{10}$ **P**	5 $+9$ $\overline{14}$ **I**	6 $+8$ $\overline{14}$ **P**	4 $+6$ $\overline{10}$ **S**

P I G   P A L S I
$\overline{14}$ $\overline{12}$ $\overline{9}$ $\overline{14}$ $\overline{11}$ $\overline{13}$ $\overline{10}$

This Takes the Cake!

Name _____ Date _____

Read each big number.
Circle 4 ways to make that number.

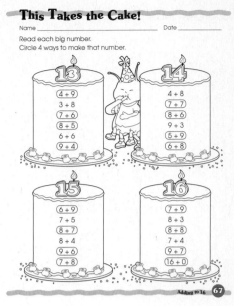

13
$4 + 9$
$3 + 8$
$7 + 6$
$8 + 5$
$6 + 6$
$9 + 4$

14
$4 + 8$
$7 + 7$
$8 + 6$
$9 + 3$
$5 + 9$
$6 + 8$

15
$6 + 9$
$7 + 5$
$8 + 7$
$8 + 4$
$9 + 6$
$7 + 8$

16
$7 + 9$
$8 + 3$
$8 + 8$
$7 + 4$
$9 + 7$
$16 + 0$

Snail Mail

Name _____ Date _____

Add.
Help Snail deliver the mail.
If the answer is **12, 13,** or **14,**
color the box **green.**

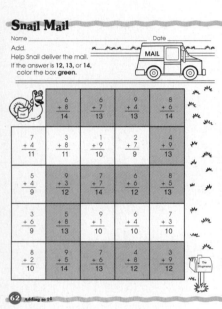

	6 $+8$ $\overline{14}$	6 $+7$ $\overline{13}$	9 $+4$ $\overline{13}$	8 $+6$ $\overline{14}$
7 $+4$ $\overline{11}$	3 $+8$ $\overline{11}$	1 $+9$ $\overline{10}$	2 $+7$ $\overline{9}$	4 $+9$ $\overline{13}$
5 $+4$ $\overline{9}$	9 $+3$ $\overline{12}$	7 $+7$ $\overline{14}$	6 $+6$ $\overline{12}$	8 $+5$ $\overline{13}$
3 $+6$ $\overline{9}$	5 $+8$ $\overline{13}$	9 $+1$ $\overline{10}$	6 $+4$ $\overline{10}$	7 $+3$ $\overline{10}$
8 $+2$ $\overline{10}$	9 $+5$ $\overline{14}$	7 $+6$ $\overline{13}$	4 $+8$ $\overline{12}$	3 $+9$ $\overline{12}$

Sweet Dreams!

Name _____ Date _____

Add.
Color by the code.

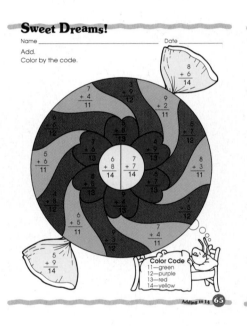

Color Code
11—green
12—purple
13—red
14—yellow

High-Flying Facts

Name _____ Date _____

Add.
Cross off a matching answer.

12	12	13	13	13	14	14
14	14	15	15	16	16	16

5 $+9$ $\overline{14}$ 7 $+9$ $\overline{16}$ 8 $+5$ $\overline{13}$ 4 $+7$ $\overline{13}$ 4 $+8$ $\overline{12}$ 3 $+9$ $\overline{12}$ 9 $+7$ $\overline{16}$ 8 $+7$ $\overline{15}$

6 $+9$ $\overline{15}$ 7 $+7$ $\overline{14}$ 4 $+9$ $\overline{13}$ 8 $+6$ $\overline{14}$ 8 $+8$ $\overline{16}$ 7 $+6$ $\overline{13}$ 5 $+8$ $\overline{13}$ 7 $+8$ $\overline{15}$

At the "Moo-vies"

Name _____ Date _____

Add.
Cross off a matching answer.

5 $+9$ $\overline{14}$	0 $+9$ $\overline{9}$	6 $+6$ $\overline{12}$	4 $+7$ $\overline{11}$	7 $+7$ $\overline{14}$	6 $+4$ $\overline{10}$
6 $+7$ $\overline{13}$	3 $+4$ $\overline{7}$	4 $+5$ $\overline{9}$	5 $+2$ $\overline{7}$	3 $+8$ $\overline{11}$	2 $+6$ $\overline{8}$
4 $+8$ $\overline{12}$	9 $+1$ $\overline{10}$	5 $+8$ $\overline{8}$	0 $+8$ $\overline{8}$	7 $+5$ $\overline{12}$	6 $+1$ $\overline{7}$
8 $+3$ $\overline{11}$	7 $+2$ $\overline{9}$	9 $+5$ $\overline{14}$	6 $+2$ $\overline{8}$	4 $+9$ $\overline{13}$	5 $+5$ $\overline{10}$

Answers

The One That Got Away!

Name _____ Date _____

Add.

$5 + 9 = 14$
$9 + 5 = 14$
$6 + 7 = 13$
$7 + 6 = 13$
$4 + 7 = 11$
$7 + 4 = 11$
$3 + 9 = 12$
$9 + 3 = 12$
$3 + 8 = 11$
$8 + 3 = 11$
$5 + 6 = 11$
$4 + 9 = 13$
$9 + 4 = 13$
$6 + 8 = 14$
$8 + 6 = 14$
$8 + 5 = 13$
$5 + 8 = 13$
$7 + 5 = 12$
$5 + 7 = 12$
$4 + 8 = 12$
$8 + 4 = 12$
$2 + 9 = 11$
$9 + 2 = 11$

And the Winner Is...

Name _____ Date _____

Add.
Color by the code.

FINISH

Color Code
11—blue 14—orange
12—red 15—green
13—purple 16—yellow

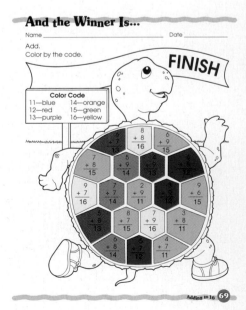

8 $+8$ $\overline{16}$
6 $+7$ $\overline{13}$
9 $+6$ $\overline{15}$
8 $+7$ $\overline{15}$
9 $+5$ $\overline{14}$
8 $+8$
9 $+6$ $\overline{15}$
9 $+7$ $\overline{16}$
7 $+7$ $\overline{14}$
8 $+7$ $\overline{15}$
9 $+7$ $\overline{16}$
7 $+9$ $\overline{16}$
8 $+7$ $\overline{15}$
7 $+9$ $\overline{16}$
3 $+8$ $\overline{11}$
5 $+8$ $\overline{13}$
8 $+6$ $\overline{14}$
4 $+7$ $\overline{11}$

Dressed and Ready to Go!

Name _____ Date _____

Add.
Color by the code.

Color Code
12—red   14—green
13—yellow 15—blue
16—purple

That's "Bear-y" Funny!

Name _____ Date _____

Add.
Write the matching letters from the code.
Read the riddle answer.

🐾 What do you call a bear with no shoes?

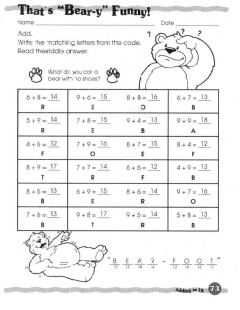

6 + 8 = 14 R	9 + 6 = 15 E	8 + 8 = 16 O	6 + 7 = 13 B
5 + 9 = 14 R	7 + 8 = 15 E	9 + 4 = 13 B	9 + 9 = 18 A
4 + 8 = 12 F	9 + 7 = 16 O	5 + 8 = 13 E	8 + 4 = 12 F
8 + 9 = 17 T	7 + 7 = 14 R	6 + 6 = 12 F	4 + 9 = 13 B
8 + 5 = 13 B	6 + 9 = 15 E	8 + 6 = 14 R	9 + 7 = 16 O
7 + 6 = 13 B	9 + 8 = 17 T	9 + 5 = 14 R	5 + 8 = 13 B

"B E A R - F O O T"
13 15 18 4   12 16 16 17

Hungry Little Rabbit!

Name _____ Date _____

Read.
Add.
Color by the code.

Color Code
11—yellow
12, 13, or 14—green
15—orange
16—red
17 or 18—brown

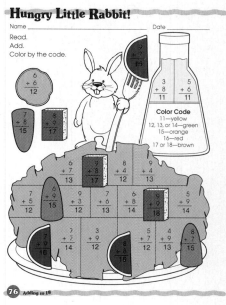

Dino Drive-In

Name _____ Date _____

Write the math sentence.

8 cars are at the movie. 8 more come. How many cars in all? 8 + 8 = 16	The dinosaur eats 6 hot dogs. He eats 9 more. How many hot dogs in all? 6 + 9 = 15
7 dinosaurs are in a car. 9 more dinosaurs join them. How many dinosaurs in all? 7 + 9 = 16	9 cars are white. 5 cars are black. How many cars in all? 9 + 5 = 14
The dinosaurs watch 6 movies. They watch 8 more movies. How many movies in all? 6 + 8 = 14	The dinosaur buys 8 drinks. He buys 7 more drinks. How many drinks in all? 8 + 7 = 15

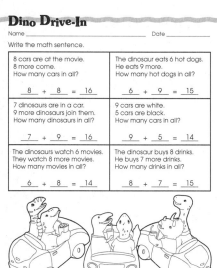

Hurry On Home!

Name _____ Date _____

Add.
Help Raccoon get home for dinner.
If the answer is 16, 17, or 18, color the box brown.

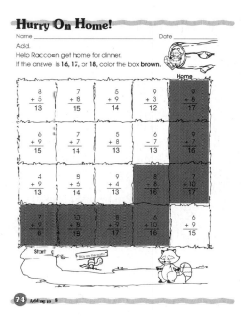

Start   Stay on the path!   Home

Yum! Cookies and Milk

Name _____ Date _____

Add.
Cross out the matching answer.

12 15 14 16 13
6 + 6 = 12
4 + 9 = 13
5 + 9 = 14
7 + 8 = 15
7 + 9 = 16

18 15 13 14 15
8 + 7 = 15
9 + 9 = 18
6 + 9 = 15
7 + 7 = 14
8 + 5 = 13

17 15 14 13 16
9 + 8 = 17
9 + 6 = 15
8 + 8 = 16
5 + 8 = 13
9 + 5 = 14

16 14 17 13 14
8 + 6 = 14
9 + 7 = 16
6 + 8 = 14
8 + 9 = 17
9 + 4 = 13

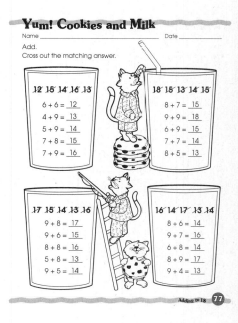

Choo! Choo!

Name _____ Date _____

Write the math sentence.

There are 7 train cars. 8 more train cars come. How many train cars in all? 7 + 8 = 15	The train drives 6 miles. It drives 9 more miles. How many miles in all? 6 + 9 = 15
7 horses are on the train. 7 more horses come. How many horses in all? 7 + 7 = 14	There are 7 boxcars. There are 9 more boxcars. How many boxcars in all? 7 + 9 = 16
The horses ride for 6 days. They ride for 8 more days. How many days in all? 6 + 8 = 14	The horse rings the bell 8 times. Then he rings it 8 more times. How many rings in all? 8 + 8 = 16

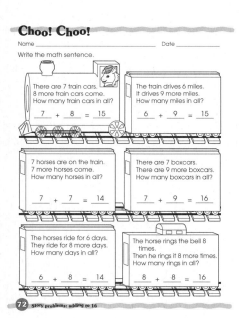

Really! It's True!

Name _____ Date _____

Read.
Add.
Color by the code.

Color Code
10 or 11—orange
12, 13, 14, 15, 16, 17, or 18—green

How many stomachs does a cow have?

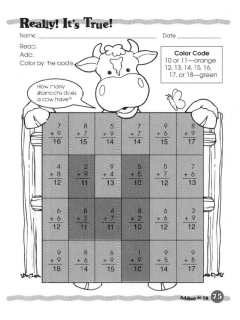

Can I Ride in the Buggy?

Name _____ Date _____

Read.
Write the math sentence.

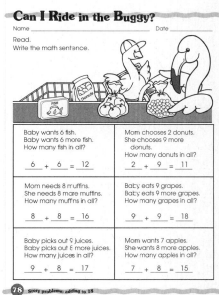

Baby wants 6 fish. Baby wants 6 more fish. How many fish in all? 6 + 6 = 12	Mom chooses 2 donuts. She chooses 9 more donuts. How many donuts in all? 2 + 9 = 11
Mom needs 8 muffins. She needs 8 more muffins. How many muffins in all? 8 + 8 = 16	Baby eats 9 grapes. Baby eats 9 more grapes. How many grapes in all? 9 + 9 = 18
Baby picks out 9 juices. Baby picks out 8 more juices. How many juices in all? 9 + 8 = 17	Mom wants 7 apples. She wants 8 more apples. How many apples in all? 7 + 8 = 15

Strike!

Name _____ Date _____

Add.
Color by the code.

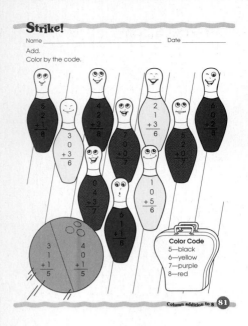

Color Code
5—black
6—yellow
7—purple
8—red

Just Hanging Around

Name _____ Date _____

Add.
Color by the code.

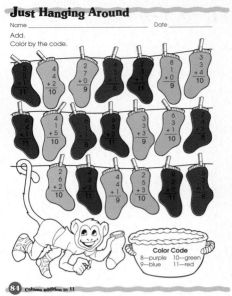

Color Code
8—purple 10—green
9—blue   11—red

Dinosaur Ditty

Name _____ Date _____

Add.
Color by the code.

Color Code
12—red 13—yellow 14—blue
15—green 16—orange

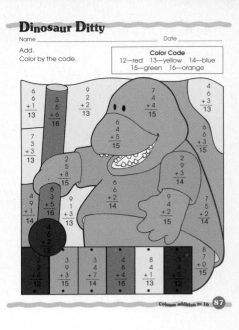

Musical Mouse Melody

Name _____ Date _____

Add.
Color by the code.

Color Code
6—brown   8—yellow
7—blue   9—black

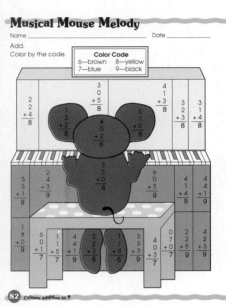

A Wild Ride!

Name _____ Date _____

Ride the roller coaster.
If the answer is 11 or 12, color the track.

The Panther Blaster

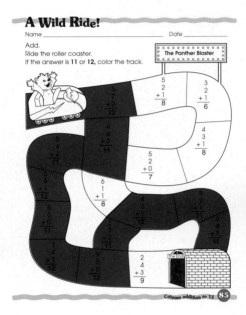

the End

A Musical Mummy Mystery

Name _____ Date _____

Add.
If the answer is 18, color it red.

What is a mummy's
favorite kind of music?

A Froggy Wedding

Name _____ Date _____

Add.
Write the matching letters from the code.
Read the riddle answer.

What do frogs do after
they get married?

Code
1 — a
2 — i
3 — v
4 — h
5 — y
6 — p
7 — r
8 — t
9 — l
10 — e

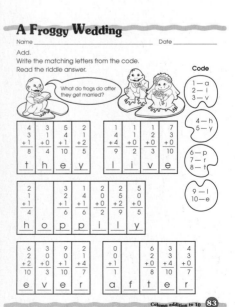

they
live
hoppily
ever after

High-Flying Numbers

Name _____ Date _____

Add.
Color a matching answer.

Lookin' Good!

Name _____ Date _____

Add.
Match the letters to the numbered
lines below to solve the riddle.

What do you call
a girl cow?

A C O W G I R L I

Oh, Good! The Math Channel!

Name _____ Date _____

Add.
Color the matching answer.

$\begin{array}{r}1\\+2\\\hline 3\end{array}$	$\begin{array}{r}3\\+2\\\hline 5\end{array}$	$\begin{array}{r}5\\+2\\\hline 7\end{array}$	$\begin{array}{r}7\\+2\\\hline 9\end{array}$
$\begin{array}{r}2\\+2\\\hline 4\end{array}$	$\begin{array}{r}4\\+2\\\hline 6\end{array}$	$\begin{array}{r}6\\+2\\\hline 8\end{array}$	$\begin{array}{r}8\\+2\\\hline 10\end{array}$
$\begin{array}{r}9\\+2\\\hline 11\end{array}$	$\begin{array}{r}11\\+2\\\hline 13\end{array}$	$\begin{array}{r}13\\+2\\\hline 15\end{array}$	$\begin{array}{r}15\\+2\\\hline 17\end{array}$
$\begin{array}{r}10\\+2\\\hline 12\end{array}$	$\begin{array}{r}12\\+2\\\hline 14\end{array}$	$\begin{array}{r}14\\+2\\\hline 16\end{array}$	$\begin{array}{r}16\\+2\\\hline 18\end{array}$

92 Adding 2

Double Trouble

Name _____ Date _____

Add.
Circle each answer in the picture

$2 + 2 = \underline{4}$

$7 + 7 = \underline{14}$

$5 + 5 = \underline{10}$

$1 + 1 = \underline{2}$

$9 + 9 = \underline{18}$

$6 + 6 = \underline{12}$

$4 + 4 = \underline{8}$

$8 + 8 = \underline{16}$

$3 + 3 = \underline{6}$

Doubles to 18 95

Under the Big Top

Name _____ Date _____

Add.

Doubles	Doubles + 1	Doubles + 2
$3 + 3 = \underline{6}$	$3 + 4 = \underline{7}$	$3 + 5 = \underline{8}$
$5 + 5 = \underline{10}$	$5 + 6 = \underline{11}$	$5 + 7 = \underline{12}$
$7 + 7 = \underline{14}$	$7 + 8 = \underline{15}$	$7 + 9 = \underline{16}$
$1 + 1 = \underline{2}$	$1 + 2 = \underline{3}$	$1 + 3 = \underline{4}$
$4 + 4 = \underline{8}$	$4 + 5 = \underline{9}$	$4 + 6 = \underline{10}$
$6 + 6 = \underline{12}$	$6 + 7 = \underline{13}$	$6 + 8 = \underline{14}$
$2 + 2 = \underline{4}$	$2 + 3 = \underline{5}$	$2 + 4 = \underline{6}$
$8 - 8 = \underline{16}$	$8 + 9 = \underline{17}$	$8 + 10 = \underline{18}$

98 Doubles, doubles plus 1 and 2

Crunch, Crunch, Crunch

Name _____ Date _____

Add.

$\begin{array}{r}1\\+0\\\hline 1\end{array}$	$\begin{array}{r}4\\+0\\\hline 4\end{array}$	$\begin{array}{r}7\\+0\\\hline 7\end{array}$	$\begin{array}{r}10\\+0\\\hline 10\end{array}$	$\begin{array}{r}3\\+0\\\hline 3\end{array}$	$\begin{array}{r}6\\+0\\\hline 6\end{array}$
$\begin{array}{r}2\\+0\\\hline 2\end{array}$	$\begin{array}{r}5\\+0\\\hline 5\end{array}$	$\begin{array}{r}8\\+0\\\hline 8\end{array}$	$\begin{array}{r}9\\+0\\\hline 9\end{array}$	$\begin{array}{r}12\\+0\\\hline 12\end{array}$	$\begin{array}{r}14\\+0\\\hline 14\end{array}$
$\begin{array}{r}11\\+0\\\hline 11\end{array}$	$\begin{array}{r}13\\+0\\\hline 13\end{array}$	$\begin{array}{r}16\\+0\\\hline 16\end{array}$	$\begin{array}{r}18\\+0\\\hline 18\end{array}$	$\begin{array}{r}15\\+0\\\hline 15\end{array}$	$\begin{array}{r}17\\+0\\\hline 17\end{array}$

Adding 0 93

It's a Luau!

Name _____ Date _____

Add.

$\begin{array}{r}3\\+4\\\hline 7\end{array}$ $\begin{array}{r}2\\-3\\\hline 5\end{array}$

$\begin{array}{r}4\\+5\\\hline 9\end{array}$ $\begin{array}{r}1\\+2\\\hline 3\end{array}$

$\begin{array}{r}5\\+6\\\hline 11\end{array}$ $\begin{array}{r}6\\+7\\\hline 13\end{array}$

96 Doubles plus 1

Page 103
Checkup 1
Test A
A. 5, 3, 4, 5, 3
B. 4, 5, 3, 4, 4
C. 5, 4, 5, 3, 5
D. 2, 1, 2, 2, 1
E. 4, 4, 4, 5, 5

Test B
A. 3, 4, 5, 4, 5
B. 3, 3, 5, 4, 5
C. 5, 4, 4, 3, 5
D. 1, 2, 2, 1, 2
E. 5, 5, 5, 3, 5

Make Mine a Double!

Name _____ Date _____

Add.
Color each ice cream by the code.

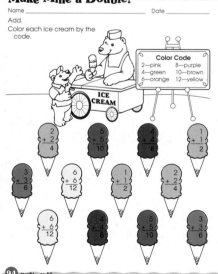

Color Code
2—pink   8—purple
4—green   10—brown
6—orange   12—yellow

$\begin{array}{r}2\\+2\\\hline 4\end{array}$ $\begin{array}{r}5\\+5\\\hline 10\end{array}$ $\begin{array}{r}4\\+4\\\hline 8\end{array}$ $\begin{array}{r}1\\+1\\\hline 2\end{array}$

$\begin{array}{r}3\\+3\\\hline 6\end{array}$ $\begin{array}{r}6\\+6\\\hline 12\end{array}$ $\begin{array}{r}1\\+1\\\hline 2\end{array}$ $\begin{array}{r}2\\+2\\\hline 4\end{array}$

$\begin{array}{r}6\\+6\\\hline 12\end{array}$ $\begin{array}{r}4\\+4\\\hline 8\end{array}$ $\begin{array}{r}5\\+5\\\hline 10\end{array}$ $\begin{array}{r}3\\+3\\\hline 6\end{array}$

94 Doubles to 12

All Lights Aglow!

Name _____ Date _____

Add.

Doubles	Doubles + 1
$2 + 2 = \underline{4}$	$2 + 3 = \underline{5}$
$6 + 6 = \underline{12}$	$6 + 7 = \underline{13}$
$3 + 3 = \underline{6}$	$3 + 4 = \underline{7}$
$8 + 8 = \underline{16}$	$8 + 9 = \underline{17}$
$4 + 4 = \underline{8}$	$4 + 5 = \underline{9}$
$1 + 1 = \underline{2}$	$1 + 2 = \underline{3}$
$7 + 7 = \underline{14}$	$7 + 8 = \underline{15}$
$5 + 5 = \underline{10}$	$5 + 6 = \underline{11}$

Doubles, doubles plus 1 97

Page 105
Checkup 2
Test A
A. 1, 4, 6, 2, 6
B. 2, 6, 4, 3, 5
C. 3, 3, 6, 4, 1
D. 6, 2, 5, 5, 3
E. 6, 2, 4, 6, 5

Test B
A. 6, 3, 4, 6, 3
B. 6, 6, 5, 4, 6
C. 5, 2, 3, 2, 6
D. 5, 4, 3, 1, 5
E. 6, 6, 6, 2, 6

Page 107
Checkup 3
Test A
A. 7, 5, 5, 2, 7
B. 6, 7, 4, 7, 4
C. 7, 3, 6, 7, 5
D. 7, 6, 5, 7, 6
E. 4, 6, 7, 7, 7

Test B
A. 7, 6, 3, 2, 7
B. 5, 7, 6, 7, 4
C. 7, 7, 6, 5, 7
D. 6, 4, 4, 5, 7
E. 7, 7, 7, 5, 5

Page 109
Checkup 4
Test A
A. 3, 7, 8, 8, 8
B. 4, 5, 8, 6, 1
C. 6, 8, 4, 7, 2
D. 5, 6, 8, 3, 7
E. 8, 5, 8, 8, 7

Test B
A. 4, 5, 6, 8, 3
B. 3, 1, 7, 5, 8
C. 8, 8, 4, 8, 7
D. 6, 7, 8, 2, 6
E. 4, 7, 8, 7, 8

Page 111
Checkup 5
Test A
A. 9, 8, 7, 7, 9
B. 9, 9, 6, 9, 8
C. 9, 8, 8, 9, 9
D. 6, 9, 9, 6, 7
E. 8, 8, 8, 8, 7

Test B
A. 9, 8, 6, 6, 8
B. 8, 9, 9, 7, 8
C. 9, 9, 8, 7, 9
D. 9, 7, 9, 6, 9
E. 9, 8, 8, 8, 6

Page 113
Checkup 6
Test A
A. 9, 10, 7, 10, 6
B. 10, 7, 10, 10, 9
C. 7, 9, 10, 9, 8
D. 10, 8, 9, 7, 10
E. 8, 10, 8, 10, 8

Test B
A. 8, 10, 8, 10, 8
B. 9, 10, 6, 9, 8
C. 10, 7, 9, 10, 10
D. 8, 9, 10, 7, 10
E. 7, 10, 10, 9, 10

Page 115
Checkup 7
Test A
A. 9, 11, 11, 9, 10
B. 9, 11, 10, 11, 10
C. 11, 10, 11, 10, 11
D. 8, 8, 11, 9, 11
E. 8, 10, 9, 9, 9

Test B
A. 8, 11, 10, 9, 11
B. 10, 11, 10, 9, 11
C. 11, 10, 11, 10, 9
D. 9, 11, 8, 11, 10
E. 9, 9, 10, 8, 8

Page 117
Checkup 8
Test A
A. 10, 12, 11, 10, 12
B. 11, 9, 12, 9, 10
C. 8, 10, 12, 7, 8
D. 12, 8, 11, 10, 12
E. 11, 8, 9, 12, 10

Test B
A. 10, 12, 11, 11, 9
B. 10, 11, 10, 10, 12
C. 12, 10, 11, 12, 11
D. 8, 11, 8, 12, 9
E. 8, 9, 12, 10, 12

Page 119
Checkup 9
Test A
A. 14, 12, 12, 14, 11
B. 11, 13, 11, 14, 13
C. 12, 13, 14, 12, 13
D. 14, 11, 13, 13, 12
E. 10, 10, 9, 12, 12

Test B
A. 13, 13, 10, 12, 14
B. 12, 12, 14, 11, 11
C. 13, 14, 11, 13, 13
D. 14, 10, 13, 10, 14
E. 10, 10, 11, 9, 12

Page 121
Checkup 10
Test A
A. 14, 13, 15, 12, 14
B. 15, 13, 12, 12, 16
C. 15, 13, 14, 14, 13
D. 14, 12, 16, 11, 13
E. 15, 13, 11, 11, 16

Test B
A. 13, 15, 14, 12, 16
B. 14, 13, 15, 13, 14
C. 16, 11, 11, 14, 15
D. 14, 13, 16, 13, 12
E. 12, 13, 12, 15, 11

Page 123
Checkup 11
Test A
A. 15, 14, 13, 15, 16
B. 14, 18, 13, 15, 14
C. 13, 16, 14, 13, 16
D. 15, 13, 17, 14, 13
E. 12, 12, 17, 11, 12

Test B
A. 15, 13, 13, 18, 15
B. 14, 16, 13, 14, 17
C. 15, 16, 14, 14, 15
D. 13, 17, 14, 13, 16
E. 12, 11, 12, 11, 12